THE SPLENDID LITTLE WAR

D0831895

FRANK FREIDEL

BURFORD BOOKS

Printed in the United States of America.

10 9 8 7 6 5 4 3 2 1

Library of Congress Cataloging-in-Publication Data
Freidel, Frank Burt.
    The splendid little war / by Frank Freidel.
        p.   cm.
    Originally published: Boston : Little, Brown, 1958.
    Includes bibliographical references.
    ISBN 1-58080-093-9
    1. Spanish-American War, 1898. I. Title.
E715.F7   2001
973.8'9—dc21   2001043258

Contents

Foreword

The Spanish-American War lasted a little less than four months in 1898. One hundred and one years later, the United States again fought a conflict that lasted only a matter of months. The nation had developed from a fledgling world power to become the world's sole superpower, yet certain parallels are evident between the Spanish-American War and that fought in Serbia. In both cases, humanitarian concerns played a key role in the decision to commit American military force. In both cases as well, American political leaders deemed the trouble spots to be "vital" interests—Cuba was a significant source of American trade and investment, and chaos in Kosovo threatened to spill into neighboring Balkan states and disrupt "peace and security" in Europe.

America's military effort in Operation Allied Force could also draw parallels to the war a century before in Cuba, the

Philippines, and Puerto Rico. In Kosovo, the United States relied on its technological edge, air power, to fight a seventy-eight-day conflict in which not a single airman was killed. In similar fashion, America turned to its relative advantage in sea power to win lopsided and near bloodless victories over the Spanish. In the battle of Manila Bay, Commodore George Dewey's Asiatic Squadron lost a single sailor in demolishing the Spanish opposition, while in the attack on the Spanish fleet attempting to escape from Santiago, the Americans used their 12- and 13-inch guns (the best the Spanish had were 11-inch) to wreck every Spanish ship at the cost of one man.

The end of both conflicts also did not result in the termination of America's military involvement in the regions where it had fought. The victory of American ground forces in the Philippines—orchestrated by the American and Spanish commanders so that the fighting would produce minimum casualties—spurred a bitter three-year guerrilla struggle by Filipino insurgent leader Emilio Aguinaldo that cost more American lives than had the Spanish-American War. In Kosovo, Serbia's capitulation to the NATO coalition resulted in the establishment of a thirty-six-thousand-man peacekeeping force to which the United States has contributed fifty-five hundred troops. That operation has continued now for more than two years, with no solid prospect for an end date.

Such parallels can be taken too far, of course, yet they do reveal much about America's approach to war during the past century. Americans have traditionally blended humanitarian concerns with the notion of vital interests as reasons for going to war; humanitarian values alone generally provide an insufficient rationale for Americans to fight. Once they do fight, they have aimed to do so as efficiently as possible—that is, they have tried to make maximum use of any technological advantage they might have, and they have tried to use that technology to keep American casualties to a minimum. That is not to say that

Americans have always succeeded in those endeavors. As Frank Freidel's account graphically illustrates, the technological advantages that the Americans had over the Spanish were at sea, not on land, and even those advantages were relative. Dewey's ships that wrecked the Spanish fleet were no match for the five German warships that arrived to scout Manila Bay soon after his victory. On the land, Americans fought with black-powder arms that revealed their positions while the Mausers used by the Spanish were smokeless. When the attacks against dug-in Spanish forces on El Caney, and San Juan and Kettle Hills, produced heavy casualties, the American commander, General William Shafter, refused to order further assaults against Spanish positions protecting Santiago and chose instead to lay siege to the Cuban city. This strategy, combined with the navy's victory over the Spanish fleet, resulted in a Spanish surrender.

Frank Freidel's narrative is a superb summary of what the war was like for the soldiers and sailors who endured it. Written while Freidel taught at Harvard, and in the midst of his six-volume magnum opus dissecting Franklin Roosevelt's presidency, the book is a combat history that relies heavily on memoirs and other first-person accounts from participants. As such, the work differs substantially from two other "classic" studies of the Spanish-American War: Walter Millis's *The Martial Spirit* (Cambridge, MA: Riverside Press, 1931) and David Trask's *The War with Spain in 1898* (New York: Macmillan Publishing Company, Inc., 1981). Both Millis and Trask present the war in its broader context, focusing on its origins and diplomacy rather than mainly combat operations. While Freidel does not completely ignore other aspects of the conflict, clearly his focus is on warfighting. He notes that his book will provide American readers with "the idealism, fortitude, and even the heroism of the tens of thousands of their fellows who sought to free Cuba and destroy Spanish power in Puerto Rico and the Philippines in 1898."

A parade of famous—and soon to be famous—Americans from the turn of the century fills Freidel's pages. The ebullient Teddy Roosevelt leads his Rough Riders up Kettle Hill, while war correspondent Steven Crane and combat artist Frederic Remington try to maintain their cool under Spanish shelling. William Jennings Bryan becomes a colonel in a Nebraska regiment that the McKinley administration never allows to get closer to Cuba than Florida. Clara Barton arrives at General Shafter's headquarters to oversee the Red Cross effort. The future commander of the American Expeditionary Force in World War I, John J. Pershing, leads troopers of the Black Tenth Cavalry Regiment into battle. Two World War II admirals, William D. Leahy and William F. Halsey, serve in naval operations off Cuba.

Yet Freidel's narrative is much more than a "who's who" of American military exploits. Many of the personal accounts referenced come from unfamiliar names. Readers will nonetheless identify with Freidel's storytellers, and will no doubt shake their heads as they learn of an American army fighting in woolen uniforms in Cuba's tropical heat, with haphazard logistical support that kept it only a few days from starvation, and without basic sanitation in an environment already prone to disease. As Freidel continually points out, many American successes resulted from Spanish ineptitude or just plain luck; the United States military was still a long way from becoming a world-class force in 1898.

Following the war, the American military would correct some of the ills that had plagued it during the conflict. In 1900 Navy Secretary John D. Long would create a General Board of senior officers to coordinate war-planning and building programs. President Theodore Roosevelt, who parlayed his assault on Kettle Hill into a New York governorship and the vice-presidency, would send his "Great White Fleet" on a dramatic cruise around the world in 1907–1909, and by World War I only the Royal Navy and the German High Seas fleet were superior to the American navy. Meanwhile, the reformist Secretary of War Elihu Root would create an Army General Staff and establish an Army War College in 1903. Although the regular army increased its strength to more than a hundred thousand men on the eve of World War I, it remained woefully behind the Europeans in terms of both manpower and equipment. Still, the Spanish-American War provided the impetus for transforming the American military into a force that could accomplish more than simply home defense.

Few Americans are likely aware of that legacy. Freidel asserts that for most Americans in 1958, when the book was first published, the conflict with Spain was largely forgotten, remembered only by John Hay's label as "a splendid little war." Freidel's assessment remains true today. Hopefully, the reprinting of his classic account will shed light on a war that helped to shape America's approach to world affairs in the modern era. At the very least, it should show that the character and conduct of the war, for those who fought it, were anything but "little" or "splendid."

—Mark Clodfelter
The National War College
July 2001

U.S.S. Maine *entering Havana Harbor*

1

Remember the *Maine*

As the Spanish-American War approached its end in the summer of 1898, the United States ambassador to England, John Hay, wrote Colonel Theodore Roosevelt of the Rough Riders:

"It has been a splendid little war, begun with the highest motives, carried on with magnificent intelligence and spirit, favored by that fortune which loves the brave."

The war was indeed splendid for most of the excited American populace far from battle areas, reading in huge headlines of one sensational act of heroism and spectacular triumph after another. But for some of the sailors, certainly for sweltering stokers, and for many of the soldiers, especially those in regiments decimated before Santiago, it was as grim, dirty, and bloody as any war in history. It was a little war, but only the incredible ineptitude of the Spaniards and the phenomenal luck of the Americans kept it from stretching into a struggle as long and full of disasters as the Boer War became for the British.

Already in 1898, the technical age was so far advanced and the power struggle among the great nations was becoming so intense that beyond the "splendid little war" hung the indefinite shadow of world cataclysm. Americans, secure in the illusion of isolation from European quarrels, idealistic in their championing of underdogs, or ambitious for their nation to assume the attributes of a great power, welcomed war with Spain. Few of them dreamed how different the United States would be afterward, and indeed many did not realize until years later what great changes had been wrought by the events of 1898 and early 1899.

It was a nation innocent of the nature of modern warfare and with little inkling of world-power politics that so boldly and idealistically set forth to punish Spain for her mistreatment of her Cuban colony. In ensuing years, with the innocence destroyed, the war seemed less than a crusade and far from splendid. Shocking revelations of the inadequacies of the War Department and even the navy, ridiculous quarrels among rival commanders, the imperial spoils with which the United States emerged, and even the relative bloodlessness and brevity of the conflict gave the Spanish-American War something of a disreputable and quasi-comic-opera aspect. The slogans, aspirations, and chivalry of the combatants seemed as quaintly antique as gaslight.

In jeering at what had been spurious or ridiculous, Americans unfortunately overlooked the idealism, fortitude, and even the heroism of the tens of thousands of their fellows who sought to free Cuba and destroy Spanish power in Puerto Rico and the Philippines in 1898. This book is their story.

How was it that the United States went to war with Spain? The answer is full of complex uncertainties. Many of the old

familiar explanations have long since broken down under careful historical research. Basically it was a popular crusade to stop
a seemingly endless revolution which was shattering Cuba. In
the 1870's, insurrectionaries and Spanish forces had fought to
an unsatisfactory peace of exhaustion. In 1895, war had again
broken out, and again Spanish forces had endlessly chased guerrilla patriots. Young Winston Churchill had come from England
to see the war firsthand and accompanied the Spaniards on one
of their fruitless forays. The patriots were not strong enough to
win, yet not weak enough to capitulate, and the entire island
suffered. By 1898, Cuba was desolate, and newspapers reported
that some four or five hundred thousand people—a quarter of
the population—were dead, and the remainder diseased and
starving. One of the sensational papers proclaimed, "Blood on
the doorsteps." So it seemed: blood on our doorsteps, and yellow fever spreading into the southern United States, while the
war fever was rising among a moral populace wrathful over
Spanish treatment of the Cubans.

It was not the business community that was howling for
war. Nor was it instigated solely by the sensationalism of the
jingo press—even though William Randolph Hearst took credit for it as the New York *Journal's* war. Perhaps it can be attrib-
uted in part to the American restlessness in the 1890's, and in
part to a desire to see the United States function like a great
nation, complete with powerful navy and strong overseas
bases. More than these factors, it was crusading morality.
Above all, the reform element in the population—those who
had been Populists and those who became Progressives—clam-
ored for the United States to rescue the Cuban people from the
Spanish malefactors.

President William McKinley and the conservative
Republican leaders in Congress reluctantly gave way before
this pressure. Senator Henry Cabot Lodge warned McKinley,
"If the war in Cuba drags on through the summer with nothing

done we [the Republican party] shall go down in the greatest defeat ever known."

Already, in November 1897, Spain, at the urging of
President McKinley, had granted autonomy to Cuba, and it had
failed. While rebels continued to fight, pro-Spanish mobs
opposing autonomy rioted in Havana. In response to the
request of the American consul general, Fitzhugh Lee, the battleship *Maine* arrived in Havana for a "friendly visit" on January
25. The Spanish officials were cordial; everything seemed
placid. Then suddenly, on the evening of February 15, 1898, at
9:40, the *Maine* blew up, killing 260 of the crew.

The cause of the explosion was never indisputably determined, but enraged Americans did not hesitate to blame the
Spanish government—unlikely though it was thus to help precipitate a war it had been trying to avoid. "Remember the *Maine*"
became the slogan of the hour.

Excitement was great, but an able diplomatic historian,
Ernest May, points out that it was forces already in operation
that had most to do with bringing war in April 1898. Spain's
experiment with autonomy had failed. In March, President
McKinley sent three messages to the American ambassador in
Madrid which suggested in total that unless Spain gave full
independence to Cuba, he would resort to the final pressure of
turning the question over to Congress. Spain did proclaim an
armistice (which would mean little in the rainy months ahead),
but showed no sign of granting independence. The American
ambassador was optimistic that this would follow, but May
argues that the administration was well aware that his optimism
was ill based, and that only intervention by the United States
could stop the unending suffering and slaughter in Cuba.

On April 11, 1898, the president sent a message to Congress. After several days' debate, Congress passed resolutions
recognizing the independence of Cuba, disclaiming any
American intention to exercise sovereignty over the island—

A soldier's farewell; a popular cabinet photo in 1898

Assistant Secretary of the Navy Theodore Roosevelt

The New York World *a day after*

First photograph of Maine *the next morning*

tantamount to a declaration of war—and finally, on April 25, voted a war resolution.

Already on April 22, the navy had sailed to clamp a blockade around the principal ports of Cuba. Under the able administration of a competent series of secretaries, culminating in John D. Long, and through the volatile, vigorous assistant secretary, Theodore Roosevelt, it had become relatively well prepared for the conflict.

Not so with the War Department, which for several decades had done little more administer patronage and maintain a thin fighting force of twenty-six thousand officers and men, mostly in areas that had been troubled by Indians. The antiquated army ways of functioning were more to blame than the inevitable scapegoat, Secretary of War Russell A. Alger, for the scandalous, even lethal, inefficiency that married the mobilization of 1898.

President McKinley, on April 23, called for 125,000 men. There was a great rush to volunteer, even greater than the rush that same spring to the Klondike gold fields in the Yukon. Adventure was a great lure for both groups of men, but those who crowded army recruiting offices could feel with patriotic virtue that they were setting forth to right great wrongs, to rescue Cubans from the cruel and wicked grasp of the Spaniards.

2

The Battle of Manila Bay

Only five days after President McKinley signed the war resolution, the American public had a spectacular victory to celebrate and a new hero to enshrine. The Asiatic Squadron under Commodore George Dewey attacked the Spanish fleet in Manila Bay and destroyed it completely without any important damage to his ships or serious casualties.

Few had expected that the first sharp blow of the war would be struck in the Philippines. Even the president confessed that after the victory he could not have told within two thousand miles where the islands were; that he had to look for them on a globe. Nevertheless, the victory represented not only a long-laid plan of Senator Lodge and Assistant Secretary Roosevelt (as has so often been told), but also detailed preparation on the part of the Navy Department and Commodore Dewey.

"Seven hours only were required by the American Squadron to place the Philippine Archipelago at the mercy of the United States, and relieve this government of anxiety for the Pacific slope and its trans-Pacific trade," Secretary Long later wrote. "More than seven years, however, had been needed to provide the ships and perfect the personnel which accomplished this result." Since the summer of 1897, the Navy Department had been gathering data on the Spanish squadron and defenses in the Philippines. The Asiatic Squadron was reinforced, and in the fall of 1897, Dewey was sent to command it. With the aid of the Navy Department, he began to study the forces in the Philippines.

On the February afternoon that Secretary Long took off, after the destruction of the *Maine*, Acting Secretary Roosevelt sent orders to Dewey to mobilize the fleet at Hong Kong, and in the event of war attack the Spanish squadron. When Long found the dispatch on his desk the next morning, he did not rescind it, and Dewey vigorously carried out the instructions. He painted his white ships battle gray, purchased a collier, full of coal, and even arranged for an emergency base on the south China coast. As war became imminent, he waited impatiently for the cruiser *Baltimore* to arrive with ammunition; if the war declaration arrived first, he would have to leave the neutral port of Hong Kong and could not clean the cruiser's foul bottom in drydock. Just in time it came. Colonel George A. Loud of the revenue cutter *McCulloch* wrote:

"On Friday, April 22, the *Baltimore* arrived from Yokohama, and in forty-eight hours was docked, bottom scraped and repaired, painted, coaled, and provisioned, and ready for further service. It was remarkable despatch; but as a declaration of war was expected every moment, Captain Dyer did not lose an instant, and his ship was a scene of busy, bustling life, surrounded by a swarm of coal-junks, water-boats, provision-junks, and sampans, all pouring their loads aboard the *Baltimore*, the painting going on at the same time.

"The fleet was ordered to leave Hong-Kong harbor Sunday, April 24. . . . The departure . . . made no little stir in Hong-Kong, the sympathy of the English there being with us. As the *Olympia* . . . passed the English hospital-ships, they gave us three hearty cheers. . . . Three steam-launches filled with enthusiastic Americans followed us down the harbor, waving flags and wishing us God-speed."

They waved off the American fleet with serious fear of its destruction. Dewey reminisced:

"In the Hong Kong Club it was not possible to get bets, even at heavy odds, that our expedition would be a success, and this in spite of a friendly predilection among the British in our favor. I was told, after our officers had been entertained at dinner by a British regiment, that the universal remark among our hosts was to this effect: 'A fine set of fellows, but unhappily we shall never see them again.'"

John T. McCutcheon of the Chicago *Record* reported:

"At about 3 o'clock the vessels dropped anchor in Mirs Bay, which is a little land-locked harbor thirty-five miles north of Hong Kong. The four other warships, which had gone the day before, were at anchor, and the two cargo boats, the *Nanshan* and *Zafiro*, were lying off a short distance. The combined fleet seemed to be very formidable."

While the ships rode at anchor in the secluded harbor, Dewey, awaiting orders, rigorously prepared his men and ships for battle. "The afternoon was spent distributing the *Baltimore's* cargo of ammunition among the other ships," wrote Lieutenant John M. Ellicott. "Next day many spars, chests, hatch-covers and other articles of wood which could be splintered by shells were sent to the transports. Twenty-four hours later a tug arrived from Hong Kong bringing the *Raleigh's* repaired machinery and U. S. Consul [Oscar F.] Williams" from Manila.

Meanwhile in Washington, the top men in the Navy Department agreed that Dewey should at once strike the Spanish squadron, but the president did not give his consent for several days. "On Thursday, April 21, I urged this action," Long reminisced. "He thought it not quite time. But early Sunday forenoon, the 24th, I conferred with him at the White House. . . . It was a lovely, sunny, spring day, a bright contrast to the grim business in hand. We sat on a sofa, he thoughtful, his face showing a deep sense of the responsibility of the hour." McKinley gave his permission and Long cabled:

"War has commenced between the United States and Spain. Proceed at once to the Philippine Islands. Commence operations at once, particularly against Spanish fleet. You must capture vessels or destroy. Use utmost endeavors."

At two o'clock on the afternoon of April 27, the Asiatic Squadron sailed for the Philippines. Shortly after it set out, Dewey had the crews assembled so that their commanders could read to them a bombastic proclamation from the captain-general of the Philippines, Basilio Augustin Davila: "A squadron manned by foreigners, possessing neither instruction nor discipline, is preparing to come to this archipelago with the ruffianly intention of robbing us of all that means life, honor, and liberty . . . to treat you as tribes refractory to civilization, to take possession of your riches. . . . Vain designs! Ridiculous boastings!" Joseph L. Stickney of the New York *Herald*, who was acting as Dewey's aide, reported that a "roar of derisive laughter . . . went up from the whole berth deck."

Early on Saturday morning, April 30, Luzon was sighted. Stickney wrote:

"The whole squadron began its final preparations for the battle that every one knew was near at hand. Aboard the *Olympia* and *Baltimore*, and possibly some of the other ships, the sheet chain cable was 'bighted' or coiled, around the ammunition hoists so as to give them considerable protection. . . . Nets of tough, pliable manila rope, about as thick as one's little finger, were stretched beneath all the boats [to serve as splinter nets]. . . . All unnecessary material was thrown overboard . . . dangerous woodwork . . . mess chests, mess tables, ditty boxes, chairs, wardroom bulkheads, and a vast quantity of other impedimenta. . . ."

As the squadron skirted the Luzon coast, prepared for trouble, the men wondered whether the Spanish squadron were lurking in Subig Bay, the strongest natural position for defense if shore batteries had been installed there. McCutcheon chronicled the tense day:

"The *Baltimore* has now her four boilers going, and has started forward to join the *Boston* and *Concord* about fifteen miles ahead. It is believed these ships will enter Subig Bay, about thirty miles north of Manila Bay, to see whether any Spanish warships are there. . . .

"At 11:30 A.M. the squadron is about eighty miles from Manila Bay. The *Baltimore* has kept close in shore and is now below the horizon, only her smoke being visible. The flagship has signaled that the schooner overhauled by the *Zafiro* had no information to give. At 2 o'clock the distance to Subig Bay is ten miles, and to Corregidor, at the mouth of Manila Bay, about forty miles. The work of lowering the after lifeboats of the *McCulloch* down half way to the water is going on, with the object of getting them into the water as expeditiously as possible if occasion arises.

"The *Baltimore, Concord* and *Boston* are supposed to have entered Subig Bay. They cannot be seen. At about 4 o'clock a faint column of smoke in the bay marks the position of one of the ships.

"The sail of another small schooner was seen about this time and bore down toward the squadron. As it reached the mouth of the bay the *Boston* and *Concord* were sighted coming out. The *Olympia, Raleigh,* and *Petrel* steamed toward the approaching schooner. Orders came from the flagship for the *McCulloch* to send an officer on board the little vessel for information. . . . It flew the Spanish flag, but in answer to questions the captain said he had not come from Manila and did not know where the Spanish warships were. The dinghy returned and the *McCulloch* followed the fleet to the mouth of Subig Bay."

Since Subig Bay was empty, Manila Bay became the target. Stickney wrote:

"Commodore Dewey stopped his flagship and made signal for commanding officers to repair on board. When every gig had been called away, and the captain of each ship was steering in solitary state toward the *Olympia* no one needed to be told that we were on the eve of battle.

"'They're comin',' said one of the old seamen, 'to hear the "old man's" last word before we go at the Dons.'

"'Not his last word,' said one of the younger men.

"'Perhaps not his,' was the reply, 'but it's near our last words some of us are. There'll be many an eye will look at that sunset to-night that'll never see another.'

"But such prophets of sorrow were rare. . . .

"The war council was of short duration. Commodore Dewey had decided on his plans before it met, and he took little time in giving to each captain his duties for the night and the next day. By seven o'clock the gigs were all hoisted at their davits, the flagship was again under way, and long before dark every vessel had taken her station, ready to run by the batteries at the mouth of the bay or to fight her passage, as circumstances might require. Aside from one light at the very stern of each ship, intended as a guide for the next in line, not a glimmer was to be seen aboard any craft in the fleet. As I looked astern from the *Olympia's* taffrail, I could just get a faint suggestion of a ghostly shape where the *Baltimore* grimly held her course on our port quarter. . . .

"The moon had risen, and although it was occasionally obscured by light clouds, the night was not one in which a squadron ought to have been able to run through a well-defended channel without drawing upon herself a hot fire. Consequently, at a quarter to ten o'clock, the men were sent to their guns, not by the usual bugle call, but by stealthily whispered word of mouth." McCutcheon on the *McCulloch* reported:

"About 11:30 the entrance to the bay can be seen. Two dark headlands—one on either side of the entrance—show up gloomy. . . . In the space between a smaller mass shows where the dreaded Corregidor lies. . . . It was understood the heaviest guns of the Spanish were at Corregidor. The entrance was also said to be planted with mines, and it was known that there were torpedoes waiting for the ships. . . .

"The *Olympia* turns in and steers directly for the center of the southern and wider channel. The *Baltimore* follows and in regular order the rest of the fleet slide on through the night toward the entrance. Still there is no firing from the forts, and it is hoped that the daring maneuver may not be discovered. . . .

"About this time the soot in the funnel of the *McCulloch* caught fire and this circumstance may have revealed the movements of the fleet to the enemy. The flames shot up out of the funnel like the fire of a rolling-mill chimney. For a minute or two it burned and then settled down to the usual heavy black rolls of smoke.

"A faint light flashed up on the land and then died out. A rocket leaped from Corregidor and then all was darkness and stillness again. The nervous tension at this time was very great. Again the flames rolled forth from the *McCulloch's* funnel. . . . While it burned it made a perfect target for the enemy. Still there was no firing."

The Spanish troops manning the dangerous batteries at Corregidor watched the American fleet enter the harbor, but for inexplicable reasons did not fire. At 12:15 Sunday morning, May 1, the Spaniards fired on the fleet from the rock El Fraile and the Americans answered. Then there was quiet, and the ships steamed on. Chief Engineer Randall of the *McCulloch* collapsed—of heat prostration it was thought—and in a few minutes died. The squadron crept along the twenty-three miles to Manila, reaching there at daybreak.

There Dewey should have found the smaller, slower, less powerful Spanish squadron arrayed under the protection of the rather formidable Spanish shore batteries. The combined firepower of the Spanish guns would have been a real threat to Dewey. But Rear Admiral Patricio Montojo y Pasarón did not wish to subject the city of Manila to bombardment, so arrayed his fleet in shallow but almost unprotected waters at Cavite, several miles away. Like almost all the Spanish commanders, he was brave but utterly defeatist. Wrote Stickney:

"At four o'clock coffee and hardtack were served to the men, and the officers were glad to get the same frugal provender. The lights of Manila had long been in sight. . . . The dawn began about half-past four o'clock, when we were almost six miles from Manila. As the sun came up exactly behind the city, the shadow cast by the land obscured the harbor foreground. Finally we made out the presence of a group of vessels in the port, but before five o'clock we were able to recognize them as merchant ships.

"Our cruisers were now in close battle order, the flagship leading, followed by the *Baltimore*, the *Raleigh*, the *Petrel*, the *Concord*, and the *Boston*." As the fleet passed Manila, the shore batteries fired several shots. Lieutenant Bradley A. Fiske on the *Petrel* recalled:

"I was aroused from my sleep by a noise at my door and a voice saying, 'The Captain wishes to see you on the bridge.' 'What about?' I said sleepily. 'I don't know,' he said, 'but it is ten minutes to five, and they have begun to shoot at us.' Then I aroused my dormant senses and realized the fact that I was about to go into battle for the first time. When I reported to the Captain on the bridge, he simply smiled and said, 'All right.' I looked ahead in the dim morning light and saw the *Olympia*,

Admiral George Dewey in the cabin of the Olympia

Dewey, Hong Kong .

~~Secret and Confidential~~

        Order the Squadron except Monocacy to Hong
Kong. Keep full of coal. In the event of declaration war
Spain, your duty will be to see that the Spanish squadron
does not leave the Asiatic coast and then offensive operations
in Philipine Islands. Keep Olympia until further orders.

                                    Roosevelt

Roosevelt's cable to Dewey

The protected cruiser Olympia

The Olympia *in action, May 1*

Baltimore, and *Raleigh.* . . . 'The Spanish fleet is over there,' said the Captain, pointing over on our starboard side; and there could be discerned a few indistinct shapes that looked like ships." A few minutes later, Fiske was up the foremast, sighting the distance of the enemy with the stadimeter, which he had invented. "To the South, the land was lower; and there, standing out in clear relief against the bright blue sky, were the awe-inspiring forms of the ships of the Spanish fleet. The *Olympia* turned to the right and headed toward them. The *Baltimore* followed, and then the *Raleigh.* I picked up my stadimeter with no very light heart, and put it to my eye. Just then a shell, coming apparently from the direction of the city, struck the water close to the *Petrel* and exploded, throwing up an enormous quantity of water, which drenched us on the platform forty-five feet above. My assistant was a man whom I had always remarked for his extraordinary imperturbability, and for some days previous to the fight I had caught myself wondering whether his imperturbability would stand the test of battle; but I was at once reassured upon this point, for as he wiped the salt water from his face he said with his customary solemnity, 'That was pretty close, sir.' . . .

"The Captain stood on the bridge beneath me, and it was extraordinary to see this man (he was one of the most nervous men I had ever seen) so absolutely composed and unnervous. He afterwards told me that during the entire battle he had not had a single physical sensation. He was not a strong man physically, and had been on deck all night and much of the day before, and yet he went through the tremendous strain and excitement of the fight without, as he said, knowing that he had any sensations, or nerves, at all. I understood this to mean that his mind was so centered on what he had to do that he himself was only one of the things he had to manage and that he was no more interested in that thing than in the other things." The immediate object of most vital concern was, of course, the Spanish vessels.

"There were seven of them in line, as it turned out," wrote Lieutenant Carlos Gilman Calkins, navigator of the *Olympia*. "The Spanish ships were ready: they were cleared for action, and their crews animated by rounds of regulation cheers and the display of battle-flags, before the action began. The first shell came from Sangley Point and fell short by a mile or so. Extreme range was then tried and the shell splashed ineffectually, more than six miles away. These wild shots steadied our nerves. . . . Our line of advance was beaconed by columns of spray where the shells sank or soared in erratic *ricochets*. . . . The fire grew faster as we ran down our distance."

"Suddenly a shell burst directly over us," reported Stickney, who was on the bridge of the *Olympia*. "From the boatswain's mate at the after 5-inch gun came a hoarse cry. 'REMEMBER THE *MAINE!*' arose from the throats of five hundred men at the guns. . . . The *Olympia* was now ready to begin the fight.

"'You may fire when ready, Gridley,' said the Commodore, and at nineteen minutes of six o'clock, at a distance of 5,500 yards, the starboard 8-inch gun in the forward turret roared forth. Presently similar guns from the *Baltimore* and the *Boston* sent 250-pound shells hurtling toward the *Castilla* and the *Reina Cristina*.

"The Spaniards seemed encouraged to fire faster, knowing exactly our distance, while we had to guess theirs. Their ships and shore guns were making things hot for us. The piercing scream of shot was varied often by the bursting of time fuse shells, fragments of which would lash the water like shrapnel or cut our hull and rigging. One large shell that was coming straight at the *Olympia's* forward bridge fortunately fell within less than one hundred feet away. . . . Another struck the bridge gratings in line with it. A third passed just under Commodore Dewey and gouged a hole in the deck."

Lieutenant Fiske from his vantage point on the *Petrel's* mast had an excellent view of the battle:

"As is well known, the American fleet paraded back and forth before the Spanish fleet, firing as rapidly as they could with proper aim. To me in my elevated perch the whole thing looked like a performance that had been carefully rehearsed. The ships went slowly and regularly, seldom or never getting out of their relative positions, and only ceased firing at intervals when the smoke became too thick. For a long while I could not form an opinion as to which way fortune was going to decide. I could see that the Spanish ships were hit a number of times, especially the *Cristina* and *Castilla*; but then it seemed to me that our ships were hit many times also, and from the way they cut away boats from the *Raleigh* and from other signs I concluded the *Raleigh* was suffering severely. I could see projectiles falling in the water on all sides of all our ships. . . .

"Two of the ships in the Spanish column were evidently much larger than the others . . . and the Captain seemed naturally to direct the fire at them. I could see also that the Spaniards directed their firing principally at the *Olympia* and *Baltimore*, which were our largest ships. . . . I think everybody was disappointed at the great number of shots lost. Our practice was evidently much better than that of the Spaniards, but it did not seem to me that it was at all good. . . .

"About the decks of the *Petrel* things were entirely different from what I had expected. I had seen many pictures of battles and had expected great excitement. I did not see any excitement whatever. The men seemed to me to be laboring under an intense strain and to be keyed up to the highest pitch; but to be quiet, and under complete self-control, and to be doing the work of handling the guns and ammunition with that mechanical precision which is the result we all hope to get from drill."

"Often I have been asked if we were afraid," declared Joel C. Evans, gunner on the *Boston*, who supervised twenty-five men carrying ammunition to the deck. "My answer is that I never saw men as easy in mind as those below." Curiosity led the men to the portholes whenever they had an opportunity. Evans had little chance for this, "as I had to be particularly careful that no error was made in the ammunition, and that not a second was lost. What between orders for full and reduced charges, steel and shell, I was kept busy all the time." Later in the morning:

"All my men were naked except for shoes and drawers, and I wore only a cotton shirt in addition. Three in the after powder division fainted from the heat, but none of my force was overcome. The heat was really fearful. The powder smoke settled down, choking us and half blinding some, and only the love of the work kept us going. The Chinese stood the heat better than we did."

The temperature was 116 degrees in the forward berth deck; this was cool compared with the engine room, where the men claimed it was sometimes 200 degrees! It certainly felt like it. A stoker on the *Olympia*, Charles H. Twitchell, later reminisced: "The battle hatches were all battened down, and we were shut in this little hole . . . it was so hot our hair was singed. There were several leaks in the steam pipes, and the hissing hot steam made things worse. The clatter of the engines and the roaring of the furnaces made such a din it seemed one's head would burst. . . .

"We could tell when our guns opened fire by the way the ship shook; we could scarcely stand on our feet, the vibration was so great. . . . The ship shook so fearfully that the soot and cinders poured down on us in clouds. Now and then a big drop of scalding water would fall on our bare heads, and the pain was intense. One by one three of our men were overcome by the terrible heat and were hoisted to the upper deck.

"Whenever a Spanish ship would make a move toward us some of the boys on deck would shout down that they were coming for us full tilt. We knew it meant sure death if the *Olympia* got a shot through her anywhere in our vicinity. . . .

"I shall never forget those few hours. . . . It seemed to me the longest day I ever lived. I'm not anxious to go through it again, and I don't think any of the others are."

On deck, the spectacle was somewhat less frightening. Lieutenant Ellicott, intelligence officer on the *Baltimore*, wrote:

"The American squadron stood past the Spanish ships and batteries in perfect column at six knots speed, making a run of two and a half miles, then returned with starboard guns bearing. The first lap followed the five-fathom curve as marked on the charts, and each succeeding one was made a little nearer, as the soundings showed deeper water than the chart indicated. The range was thus gradually reduced [from three miles to as little as a mile]. . . .

"Under the miraculous providence which ordered the events of that day those six American ships steamed serenely back and forth unharmed for nearly three hours. . . . The pall of smoke which hung between the contending vessels prevented the effect of many shots from being seen, but close scrutiny with the glasses gave the comforting assurance after the first twenty minutes that the enemy was being hit hard and repeatedly, and as the range grew less, so that guns' crews could watch the fall of their shots with the naked eye, many an exultant cheer went up from every ship. Naked to the waist and grimy with the soot of powder, their heads bound up in water-soaked towels, sweat running in rivulets over their glistening bodies, these men who had fasted for sixteen hours now slung shell after shell and charge after charge, each within a hundred to two hundred and fifty pounds, into their huge guns . . . under a tropical sun which melted the pitch in the decks."

Two of the Spanish ships, reported Lieutenant Calkins, "were moored with springs on their cables. The others steamed about in an aimless fashion, often masking their comrades' fire, occasionally dodging back to the shelter of the arsenal and now and then making isolated and ineffectual rushes in advance— rushes which had no rational significance except as demonstrations of the point of honor. They were mere flourishes of desperation inspired by defeat."

"Toward the end of the action," wrote Ellicott, "the *Cristina* stood out as if unable to endure longer her constricted position, but the concentration of fire upon her was even greater than before, and she turned away like a steed bewildered in a storm. It was seen that she was on fire forward. Then a six-inch shell tore a jagged hole under her stern from which the smoke of another fire began to seep out. Right into this gaping wound another huge shell plunged, driving a fierce gust of flame and smoke out through ports and skylights. Then came a jet of white steam from around her after smokestack high into the air, and she swayed onward upon an irregular course toward Cavite until aground under its walls.

"The Spanish Admiral's flag was now hoisted upon the *Isla de Cuba*, and many guns were turned upon it, but the excellent target presented by the white sides of the *Castilla* held for her a large attention. Shell after shell burst in her hull, and the dark columns of smoke which followed told of deadly fires started.

"Then the *Duero* pointed her long ram out past Sangley Point, either preparing to use a torpedo or endeavoring to escape, but she received the same storm of shells as the *Cristina*, and retired on fire.

"It was now 7:30. The *Cristina* was out of action and on fire, the *Castilla's* guns were almost silenced, and all the rest of the Spanish fleet except the *Ulloa* were retiring behind the mole at Cavite Arsenal, whence they could not escape." At this point, it was erroneously reported to Commodore Dewey that ammunition was running short. "At 7:35 the flagship signalled 'Withdraw from action,' followed by 'Let the people go to breakfast.' Ten minutes later the American squadron stood out beyond the range of the persistent shore batteries and came to rest. Battle gratings were lifted and grimy men crowded on deck, clambering upon every available projection on the blistered, flame-scorched sides of their ships to cheer each other like demons released from Hades. Commanding officers were then called on board the flagship to discuss plans of final destruction."

After the conference and breakfast, the squadron steamed back to deliver a *coup de grâce* to the Spanish ships and shore fortifications. Lieutenant Ellicott wrote:

"The *Baltimore* . . . considerably in advance of the squadron . . . got safely within 2,500 yards of the beach, then turned to port at 11:05 and steamed slowly. Then followed for ten minutes a duel with the batteries which is attested by the onlooking squadron (not them within fighting distance) as one of the most magnificent spectacles of the day. The big cruiser, slowing and creeping along at a snail's pace, seemed to be in a vortex of incessant explosions both from her own guns and the enemy's shells. At times she was completely shrouded in smoke and seemed to be on fire, while every shell she fired was placed in the earthworks as accurately as if she were at target practice. Canacao battery was the first to fall under this deadly fire. Its embankments of sand, backed by boiler iron, were torn up and flung into the faces of the gunners until panic took hold of them. Hauling down their flag, they tumbled into an ambulance and drove madly to the protection of Fort Sangley. The whole fire of the squadron was then concentrated upon this fort. . . . At last . . . the Spanish flag came down and a white flag was raised in its place.

"There remained only the cruiser *Ulloa*, moored just inside Sangley Point. . . . The intrepid ship was literally riddled with shells, nearly every gun being dismounted or disabled. At length the crew swarmed over her unengaged side and swam for shore. Then she gave a slow roll toward her executioners and sank beneath the waves. . . .

"The little *Petrel* alone was able by her light draught to steam in to the arsenal, which she did with gallant dash. Those on the less fortunate ships held their breath, expecting to see her draw the fire of all the hidden Spanish gunboats, but after she had fired a few shots, which were not returned, the last Spanish flag was hauled down, and at twenty minutes after noon, a white flag was hoisted on the arsenal sheers and the *Petrel* signalled 'The enemy has surrendered.'

"Sending his chief-of-staff to the *Petrel* to receive the surrender, Commodore Dewey steamed at once to Manila, followed later by the *Baltimore, Raleigh, Concord, McCulloch* and transports. The squadron anchored off the city as unmolested as if in time of peace. The sun went down amid the usual evening concert and one could scarcely realize that he had just participated in the most complete naval victory of modern times."

The Asiatic Squadron had destroyed ten Spanish war vessels and captured the Cavite naval yard. Nearly four hundred Spanish were killed and wounded; only a few Americans were slightly injured, and not a ship seriously damaged. The utter demoralization of the Spanish was shown by the feat of the *Petrel,* whose commander, E. P. Wood, later wrote, "When the Spanish flag was hauled down at the arsenal, the *Petrel* was within three hundred yards of the arsenal dock. There she remained until 5:20 P.M., and with one boat's crew burned seven vessels of war in the face of the military garrison in Cavite."

At home, rejoicing Americans assumed the Philippines had been won, and took scant stock of the implications. And they instantly elevated Commodore Dewey to their gallery of heroes. In chromos and sculpture, his became the face of the hour.

3

As Johnny Went Marching Off

There had not been such excitement since the Civil War as the nation celebrated the victory at Manila and cheered the soldiers marching off to camp. It was war again, with all the thrills, few of the promised perils, and, to universal satisfaction, with the blue and the gray reunited.

"In April, everywhere over this good, fair land, flags were flying," wrote the Kansas editor William Allen White. "Trains carrying soldiers were hurrying . . . to the Southland; and . . . little children on fences greeted the soldiers with flapping scarfs and handkerchiefs and flags; at the stations, crowds gathered to hurrah for the soldiers, and to throw hats into the air, and to unfurl flags. . . . The fluttering of the flags drowns the voice of the tears that may be in the air. . . .

"The cheering crowds, the women bearing boughs of lilacs and garden flowers of the new spring to the car windows helped

the youths' spirits; and when they filed down the asphalt streets
of the capital and had halted in front of the State House to hear
the Governor make a speech, they were sure that it would be all
up with Spain from that hour.

"During the early weeks of May, at each State capital, several thousand young gentlemen were acquiring useful instruction in the science of arms. Many pert young militiamen came
up from the inland towns who fancied they were soldiers
because they could get across a level piece of ground without
stepping on their own feet. But after the first four or five hours
of hard work, the proud lines of the guardsmen began to sag
and then to cave in, and the enthusiastic youngsters in 'nobby'
blue clothes often found that they occupied a place in the
esteem of the regular army sergeant very little higher than the
raw men who stumbled around at their drilling in frightened,
sweaty droves."

At first it seemed rather like playing at war, as the national
guardsmen and the volunteers rushed into camp. White
reported a western governor who opposed letting his state's
militia camp in tents in a field: "But what if it rains?" It seemed
rather incredible that the Democratic presidential candidate
of 1896, William Jennings Bryan, was colonel of a Nebraska
"silver" regiment (which the administration in Washington
never allowed to get south of Florida). It was less strange that
the bellicose assistant secretary of the navy, Theodore
Roosevelt, resigned to become lieutenant colonel of a Rough
Riders regiment, which he and Colonel Leonard Wood assembled at San Antonio, Texas. But one hot afternoon after
Roosevelt had drilled one of the squadrons, he bought beer for
the men, and that evening became the object of a discourse on
discipline by Wood. "I wish to say, sir, that I agree with what
you said," Roosevelt privately told Wood a few minutes later. "I
consider myself the damnedest ass within ten miles of this
camp. Good night."

The war did not last long enough to dispel the amateurishness, and some of the troops went into battle having scarcely fired a shot. But the life in camp was hard and they quickly became toughened to it. Early May was exceptionally wet, and they all became accustomed to sleeping in the rain. They did not adjust well to the bad food, and some even were poisoned by "embalmed" or spoiled beef. Nor was sanitation ever what it should be, and diseases ranging from measles to typhoid raced through some of the camps.

President McKinley and Secretary Alger had so narrowly interpreted the expenditure of a fifty-million-dollar appropriation of March 9 "for national defence" that the War Department was not allowed to purchase or order, until war broke out, any additional modern rifles, smokeless powder, medical and hospital supplies, or other material. The volunteers had to be furnished, for a tropical campaign, heavy blue uniforms suitable for duty in Alaska and ancient Springfield carbines worse than worthless in combat.

The War Department added 182,000 volunteers to the 28,000 regulars, and divided them into seven corps. These were established at Camp Thomas (Chickamauga Park), Georgia; Camp Alger, Falls Church, Virginia; Mobile, Alabama; Tampa, Florida; and San Francisco, California. Already before war broke out, the regulars were being concentrated at Chickamauga, New Orleans, Mobile, and Tampa. One of them, M. B. Stewart, later a brigadier general, reminisced:

"Sudden orders sent regiment after regiment speeding toward southern concentration camps. . . . A brief order, a period of frenzied packing, a moment in which each donned a blue flannel shirt, exchanged cap for campaign hat, wrapped his trousers around his calves and encased them in canvas leggings, strapped on a revolver, kissed his wife, if he had one, and was ready. . . .

"One by one, regiments began to arrive in one concentration camp or another, pulled themselves together, spent a day

Company K, Ninth Massachusetts, leaving Clinton, Mass

Colonel William Jennings Bryan visiting a New Jersey regiment

Officers' mess of Rough Riders at San Antonio, Texas

Second Infantry deploying, Tampa, Fla.

Old sergeants, Second Infantry

Bathing artillery horses, Port Tampa

or so making things shipshape, then settled down to training as training was understood in those days. Organization of a kind was gradually effected but under many handicaps. With few general officers or staff officers, everything had to be extemporized. Unprepared in every sense for war, we went about our job with a cheerfulness, activity and zeal born of our own vast ignorance. Most of our efforts would have caused a modern commander to go gray overnight and would have bred hysterics in our present highly-schooled staff. However, we were dong the best we knew and our lack of knowledge was more than outweighed by the magnificent spirit and discipline of both officers and men.

"Congress, with belated energy, provided for general officers, staff officers, expansion and organization, and in due season, out of seeming chaos, brigades and divisions began to take form and substance. Gradually, also, regiments began to migrate Tampa-ward in preparation for we knew not what. Incidentally, we began to receive recruits whom we had no time to train, various articles of winter clothing, for which we had no use, and other impedimenta which were chiefly impedimenta."

For the recruits, it was a different life from what they had imagined. A Kansan in the First Illinois Cavalry wrote from Chattanooga, Tennessee:

"There is one thing distinctly noticeable about army life that the 'young patriot' soon discovers, and that is its lack of romance and the extremely practical turn given to everything. Pictures of flashing sabers and charging horses are very inspiring to look at, but an hour's saber drill with the thermometer at 105 degrees and riding horses bareback in a blinding dust three miles to water is a great deal more practical. . . . If any one who reads this thinks army life is all dress parade and enthusiasm, he must remember that there is fatigue, police, and kitchen duty to perform. Reveille sounds at 5 A.M.; every hour after that until 6:45 P.M. is occupied, when retreat is sounded. . . . I never enjoyed better health in my life than I do now. The boys are all anxious to get into active service, and I hope we will."

At the end of May as more and more of the troops began to converge as part of the Fifth Corps at Tampa, the question was when would they get into combat? The men drilled and maneuvered in the sand and palmetto, while the officers lounged and gossiped in the bizarre Moorish brick Tampa Bay Hotel. Richard Harding Davis reported:

"During the early part of May the myriads of rocking-chairs on the long porches were filled with men. This was the rocking-chair period of the war. . . . Officers who had not met in years, men who had been classmates at West Point, men who had fought together and against each other in the last war . . . were gathered together. . . . Their talk was only of an immediate advance. It was to be 'as soon as Sampson smashes the Cape Verde fleet.'"

The army trained and waited—waited for news that it could sail to Cuba without being menaced by the Spanish squadron.

U.S.S. Oregon *in 1898*

Monitor Miantonomoh at Key West

4

Hunting the Spanish Fleet

A thrill of excitement and fear ran along the eastern seaboard during the early weeks of the war, as millions of Americans wondered if they would suddenly be attacked by raiding Spanish warships. The Spanish fleet under Admiral Pascual Cervera y Topete had already assembled and was about to set forth for an unknown destination. It was rated as weaker than that of the United States, but capable of rendering serious damage, especially if it were employed in quick and devastating attacks on East Coast ports and shipping.

The British naval expert Frederick T. Jane, compiler of *Fighting Ships*, in April 1898 predicted an ultimate American triumph, especially if the two fleets met in massed combat. He commented:

"It is the people and towns upon the American coast that it will best pay Spain to damage, and the re-engined *Pelayo* should

almost be able to do this with impunity for a long while. . . .
The *Cristóbal Colón* again could do much the same thing . . . and
the other Spanish armoured ships should be more than sufficient to stop any blockade of Havana, with a view to preventing the *Pelayo* and *Colón* from returning thither to coal." If Spain
were to adopt a good strategy, "then the patriotic citizens of the
States may well come to rue the day that the meddling finger of
Uncle Sam was thrust into the hornet's nest of Cuba."

Jane was incredibly ignorant of the woeful state of the
Spanish navy, nor did he know of Admiral Cervera's gloomy
prediction that war "would mean a terrible catastrophe for poor
Spain." Yet in hindsight, even taking into account this weakness,
French E. Chadwick, who had commanded the *New York*, felt the
best Spanish strategy would have been to sail to Puerto Rico,
refuel there, then launch a raid upon the American coast. Had
Admiral Cervera possessed daring as well as courage, and had
the Spanish vessels approached anywhere near their rated twen-
ty-knot speed, New York City would have been in real danger.

To meet the demands of worried citizens for shoreline
defense, old monitors (of the Civil War design) were dispatched
to several harbors. The main tasks of the navy were to blockade
Cuban ports and to seek out and destroy Cervera's fleet.

Long before hostilities began, the Navy Department took a
step toward strengthening the North Atlantic Fleet by ordering
the first-class battleship *Oregon* to join its three sister ships in
Atlantic waters. The *Oregon* was coming out of drydock in
Bremerton, Washington, when news arrived of the sinking of
the *Maine*. It took on fuel and ammunition at San Francisco,
then left on March 19 on the eleven-thousand-mile trip
through the Straits of Magellan.

Some European experts predicted that the heavy battleship
would founder in the stormy waters of the South Atlantic, and
indeed Captain Charles E. Clark had reason to worry. They
approached the reef-strewn western entrance to the straits after

nightfall in an extreme gale. "That proved to be a very wild and stormy night—" wrote Lieutenant E. W. Eberle, "a night of great anxiety for those on watch; but with two anchors down, and engines ready for instant use, we rode out one of the most severe gales that had been experienced along that storm-swept coast for many a month."

Several weeks later, as the *Oregon* approached the Caribbean, it ran the danger of encountering the Spanish squadron. Seaman R. Cross wrote in his diary on May 7 that Captain Clark had warned all hands of the danger: "And after telling us about the fleet that was going to whip the socks off us . . . he said of course it was his duty to the Government to get the ship around on the other side and stear clear of the fleet if posable. But in case he did meet the fleet he was sure Spain's fighting efficiency on the sea would be demineshed. So we all gave him three rousen cheers and the old man Blushed, but he is dandy Just the same."

On May 26, the Oregon arrived at Key West, ready for service, having made the voyage at a speed unprecedented for a battleship—sixty-eight days.

The small naval station at Key West was rapidly expanding into the major naval base of the war. Soon a forest of masts filled the previously sleepy harbor. A flotilla of press boats came and went from the quay, attaching themselves to the warships like pilot fish to sharks. Innumerable of the blockading vessels were constantly sailing back to the harbor to refuel from the large piles of coal hastily shipped in, or to repair broken machinery at the quickly expanded shop.

On the day of the declaration of war, wrote Richard Harding Davis, Key West became "the storm-centre of the map of the United States":

"At the water's edge one could see launches, gigs, and cutters streaking the blue surface of the bay with flashes of white and brass; signal flags of brilliant reds and yellows were spread-

ing and fluttering at the signal halyards; wig-waggers beat the
air from the bridges, and across the water, from the decks of the
monitors, came the voices of the men answering the roll: 'One,
two, three, FOUR! *one, two* three, FOUR!'"

The next morning, the squadron, under Rear Admiral
William T. Sampson, was on its way to blockade Havana: "The
leaden-painted warships moved heavily in two great columns,
the battle-ships and monitors leading on the left, the cruisers
moving abreast to starboard, while in their wake and on either
flank the torpedo-boats rolled and tossed like porpoises at play."

The blockade seemed to Davis to run with remarkable efficiency during the ten days he witnessed it from the flagship
New York: "There were some exciting races after blockade-run-
ners, some heavy firing, some wonderful effects of land and sea
and sky, some instances of coolness and courage and of kind-
ness and courtesy; but what was more impressive than all else
besides, was the discipline of the ship's company and the per-
fection of her organization." On April 27, the *New York* bombarded earthworks at Matanzas, and one evening fired at some
Spanish soldiers, who had been volley-firing their rifles at the
vessel. The sailors crowded the decks to watch the spectacle,
reported Davis:

"As each shell struck home they whispered and chuckled. . . .
Meanwhile from below came the strains of the string band playing for the officer's mess. . . . This is not a touch of fiction, but
the reporting of cold coincidence, for war as it is conducted at
this end of the century is civilized."

No one was hurt, and it all seemed quite romantic in
accounts like Davis's. Ashore, American spies and agents
seemed to lead equally charmed existences. Lieutenant Henry
H. Whitney, feeling as though there were a noose around his
neck, explored Puerto Rico disguised as a seaman, then after
ten days embarked safely. Lieutenant A. S. Rowan crossed
Cuba to locate the insurgent general, Calixto García, an

exploit which Elbert Hubbard hailed in a tract distributed by the millions, glorifying blind obedience of orders. Above all, there was Ensign Henry H. Ward, who sailed a yacht with impunity into the harbors of Cadiz, the Canaries, and finally San Juan, Puerto Rico.

One of the first signs that the war could be grimmer came on May 7 when the torpedo boat *Winslow*, rashly entering Cardeñas harbor, was raked by Spanish shells, killing Ensign Worth Bagley and five sailors. Bagley was the only naval officer killed in the war.

This caused Captain J. H. Dorst to act with some caution when the Spanish soldiers tried to prevent the landing of his expedition of 120 men of the First Infantry, carrying arms and munitions for the Cubans. It was a ludicrously ill-conceived and ill-executed effort, fully heralded in advance in the newspapers, aboard an antiquated side-wheeler, the *Gussie*, well known in Havana. For hours on May 12 it sailed along the Cuban coast, chased by cavalry and fired upon from the shore. "It was apparent that the whole country was apprised of our coming and knew the purpose of it," Stephen Bonsal reported. "The heliograph stations upon the low mountains near the coast were at work signaling our presence." In the afternoon when Company E finally landed, no Cuban patriots were to be found, and the Spanish civil guard drove away the invaders. The only American casualty was a newspaper correspondent, James F. J. Archibald, wounded in the arm.

Several days later, the *Gussie* had to return ignominiously to Tampa, still carrying the supplies. Captain Dorst, who had been elevated to lieutenant colonel during his absence, blamed the fiasco upon the newspapermen. More than they were at fault for what a photographer at Tampa, D. L. Elmendorf, called "an idiotic performance . . . a disgraceful picnic."

With more secrecy and in a more satisfactory transport, the *Florida*, Colonel Dorst again set sail on May 17. This time he successfully put in at Port Banes on the north coast of Cuba, where he landed an insurgent general and over four hundred of his men, seventy-five hundred Springfield rifles, 1,300,000 rounds of ammunition, and quantities of equipment and clothing.

Meanwhile, the navy under fire had cut some but not all of the cables. From time to time it attacked Spanish fortifications or isolated gunboats or small cruisers. These forays continued throughout the war; an attack upon Manzanillo, in which Lieutenant William F. Halsey participated, was ended by the armistice. These were peripheral operations.

The paramount problem of the Navy was to locate and destroy Admiral Cervera's fleet, which had sailed from the Cape Verde Islands on April 29. The American naval vessels in the Atlantic were unwisely divided into four parts: two unimportant defensive squadrons, a Flying Squadron of several battleships and cruisers, and the Atlantic Fleet, the remainder of the capital ships. While Admiral Sampson commanded the Atlantic Fleet in the Caribbean, Commodore William S. Schley stood poised with the Flying Squadron at Hampton Roads, Virginia, to repel a coastal attack.

When Admiral Sampson learned that Cervera had departed westward, he guessed quite correctly that he would head for San Juan, Puerto Rico, to refuel. At Sampson's request, the navy sent three fast auxiliary cruisers, the *St. Louis, Harvard,* and *Yale,* to watch for the Spanish fleet at the Windward Islands where they would first appear. Sampson himself headed with the Atlantic Squadron for San Juan. He estimated that Cervera would arrive there May 8, and hoped to catch the Spanish vessels coaling and bombard them from the sea.

The voyage was a nightmare. The fast armored cruiser *New York* and the battleship *Iowa* had to crawl along at an average of less than six knots, towing two sluggish monitors, and waiting for the *Indiana,* almost disabled by bad boilers. They took eight days, twice as long as expected, to reach San Juan. Early on the morning of May 12, the Atlantic Fleet arrived, with Admiral Sampson on the *Iowa*. At 5:15, reported W. A. M. Goode:

"The bugler sounded 'Commence Firing,' and the forward 12-inch turret of the *Iowa* bellowed out its awakening call to San Juan. A second later the whole starboard side of the battleship was enveloped in smoke and vivid with jets of fire. The range varied from 2,300 to 1,100 yards. At a speed of about five knots the *Iowa* passed the harbor mouth, followed by the other ships, whose batteries opened as soon as the guns could be brought to bear. The dark hillside was dotted with the geyser-like earth-clouds of exploding shells, most of them rising around Morro and the barracks. After we once passed the harbor mouth we were certain that Cervera was not inside."

Nevertheless, Admiral Sampson continued the bombardment. The evening before, Goode had asked Sampson if he intended to take the city if Cervera were not there, "'Well,' he replied, 'if they want to give us the city, I suppose we can't refuse it.'" After three hours' bombardment, San Juan still did not surrender, so Sampson sailed off. The firing had been wild on both sides. The navy had done a little scattered damage, and killed or wounded several score people, mostly civilians. The Spanish had wounded several sailors and killed one man, Frank Widemark on the *New York*.

That same day, word came that the Spanish fleet had stopped at Martinique; Cervera, learning of Sampson's whereabouts, had avoided San Juan. The Navy Department rushed the Flying Squadron to Key West, and thence on May 18 to Cienfuegos on the south coast of Cuba. If Schley did not find Cervera there, he was to rush to Santiago, which was much further to the east. During the ten days that followed, Schley hunted for Cervera with agonizing slowness, finally arriving at Santiago on May 26. Without ascertaining whether Cervera was there, he ordered a return to Key West for coal, and for two days remained away from Santiago despite urgent orders from

Secretary Long. Finding he could refuel at sea, he did return on the late afternoon of May 28. The next morning, he saw the Spanish cruiser *Colón* anchored in plain sight in the harbor mouth—where indeed it had been on the twenty-sixth. Fortunately, Cervera, also dilatory, had not dashed out of Santiago as he had planned, early on the morning of the twenty-eighth. But it was not until June 4 that Schley determined that all of Cervera's fleet was indeed in Santiago harbor.

Admiral Sampson arrived on June 1 with the *New York* and the *Oregon,* and established a tighter blockade of Santiago harbor. He arrayed his ships in a semicircle six miles from the harbor entrance, and at night kept searchlights focused upon it. In addition, Sampson conceived a scheme to cork the harbor by sinking a large collier, the *Merrimac,* across the narrowest part of the tortuous channel. Lieutenant Richmond Pearson Hobson, an assistant naval constructor, fitted the collier with ten torpedoes which could be fired electrically, and himself led a party of seven volunteers on the difficult and dangerous assignment.

"It was an impressive night among the men of the fleet," wrote an Associated Press correspondent, "for few expected that the members of the little crew would see another sunrise. The night was cloudy, with fitful lightning flashing behind the dark lines of the hostile shore, now and then showing the grim shadows of the battlements. . . . The black hull of the *Merrimac* began to drift slowly toward the land, and in half an hour was lost to sight. It was Lieutenant Hobson's plan to steam past Morro, swinging crosswise of the channel, drop his anchors, open the valves, explode the torpedoes of the port side, leap overboard, preceded by his crew, and make his escape and theirs in a little lifeboat which was towed astern, if possible; if not to attempt to swim ashore. All the men were heavily armed, ready to make a fierce resistance to capture."

On their second start, at 3:30 on the morning of June 3, they crept within five hundred yards of the harbor entrance before the guns and musketry of the forts opened an intense fire upon them. Two ship-lengths from Morro Point, Hobson cut the engine, and the momentum carried the *Merrimac* almost to the position where she should turn and be sunk. He later described the moment:

"There was the position! 'Hard aport!' 'Hard aport, sir.' No response of the ship! 'Hard aport, I say!' 'The helm is hard aport, sir, and lashed.' 'Very well, Deignan,' I said; 'lay down to your torpedo.'

"Oh, heaven! Our steering-gear was gone, shot away at the last moment, and we were charging forward straight down the channel!" Hobson ordered the torpedoes fired, but only two of them exploded; the Spanish shellfire had shattered the batteries for detonating them.

While the vessel, out of control, slowly drifted and sank, there was nothing the crew could do but try to survive. Chief Boatswain's Mate Osborn W. Deignan remembered:

"We all lay on the deck, packed like sardines in a box, with shots flying about our heads, expecting every minute to be killed." About four o'clock, "our vessel gave a list to starboard. . . . Lieutenant Hobson, when he saw she was sinking, said, 'Very good! they are helping us out; they are doing it for us.' . . . At this time the water was pouring in over the starboard rail, coming down on us, when we scrambled to our feet and seized the rail to prevent being washed into the hold. The ship then gave a list to port, the water coming over our port rail. . . . We all leaped overboard and swam for the catamaran, which was floating near the ship's side. Just as we started for it the *Merrimac* sank, and the suction drew us down with her under the water."

For several hours they floated with only their heads above water, clinging to the catamaran. At about six o'clock, a Spanish steam launch came out, and Admiral Cervera himself helped pull Hobson and his men out of the water. That afternoon, he sent a boat under flag of truce to carry word to Sampson that the crew of the *Merrimac* were prisoners of war. Far up the channel, the men on the American ships could see the masts of the *Merrimac*, sunk but apparently not blocking the channel.

After the failure, Admiral Sampson began the frequent bombarding of the Spanish fortifications at Santiago, carefully keeping his fleet at a respectable distance from the many guns. He could not know that one of them bore the date 1668, five others, 1724, and that some of them had a range no more than eight hundred yards. They failed to damage the American fleet, and conversely, the naval bombardments caused little real destruction ashore.

As the blockade showed signs of being indefinite, Admiral Sampson felt the need to establish a nearby base in protected waters for coaling. On June 6, he sent the *Marblehead* and *Yankee* under Commander B. H. McCalla to seize the excellent lower bay at Guantánamo, about forty miles east. They drove off a Spanish gunboat, immobilized a blockhouse, and landed a hundred marines; several days later, 647 more were landed under Lieutenant Colonel Robert W. Huntington. The marines established Camp McCalla, the first base on Cuban soil, from which they protected the blockading vessels as they shuttled in from their station off Santiago to coal.

The marines engaged in the first fighting on land when Spanish troops made repeated nighttime sorties against Camp McCalla. In retaliation, the marines counterattacked, wrecked a Spanish camp, and destroyed their only fresh-water well. Stephen Crane, a correspondent with them, discovered at first hand the emotions of men under fire, about which he had written in *The Red Badge of Courage*. He described movingly the bravery of the marines and the nature of death as it came to his friend, Acting Assistant Surgeon John Blair Gibbs. As Crane lay flat one night, "feeling the hot hiss of the bullets trying to cut my hair":

"I heard somebody dying near me. He was dying hard. Hard. It took him a long time to die. He breathed as all noble machinery breathes when it is making its gallant strife against breaking, breaking. But he was going to break. . . . The darkness was impenetrable. The man was lying in some depression within seven feet of me. Every wave, vibration, of his anguish beat upon my senses. He was long past groaning. There was only the bitter strife for air which pulsed out into the night in a clear penetrating whistle with intervals of terrible silence in which I held my own breath in the common unconscious aspiration to help. I thought this man would never die. I wanted him to die. Ultimately he died. At the moment the adjutant came bustling along erect amid the spitting bullets. . . . 'Where's the doctor? There's some wounded men over there. Where's the doctor?' A man answered briskly: 'Just died this minute, sir.'"

It was an earnest of what awaited in Cuba for many an American fighting man.

Correspondents at Tampa; Stephen Crane in white suit, Richard Harding Davis in helmet

General Calixto Garcia and staff at headquarters

5

Expedition
to Cuba

God takes care of drunken
men, sailors, and the United States," quoted Richard Harding
Davis, and cited the expedition to Cuba as a severe testing of
the axiom. Even by the standards of nineteenth-century warfare
it was bizarre and risky almost beyond belief.

With Admiral Cervera's fleet located and presumably bot-
tled, it finally became the turn of the army to share in the
fighting, the headlines, and the glory, once it could get to
Cuba. But there was more recrimination than glory in the
shocking two weeks that followed the War Department order
to General William R. Shafter on May 26 to prepare to load
twenty-five thousand men and their equipment on transports at
anchor in Tampa Bay. Like a stick thrust into an anthill, it trans-
formed the relatively orderly army camps into the wildest state
of confusion.

President McKinley had in mind only a minor expedition—the one for which General Shafter had been preparing since the beginning of May. Fortunately, the utterly incompetent War Department was ready to wait until fall when the peril of yellow fever was past before sending the main armies under the commanding general of the army, Major General Nelson A. Miles, to take Havana. Most troops were to remain drilling safely in camp in Florida through the summer.

As for the minority who considered themselves highly privileged to sail for Spanish territory, they had no inkling, even in this, the most openly reported of all little wars, where their destination was to be. On May 30, the War Department sent Shafter a wire in cipher, which somehow he kept from his men and the correspondents:

"You are directed to take your command on transports, proceed under convoy of the navy to the vicinity of Santiago de Cuba, land your force at such place east or west of that point as your judgment may dictate, under the protection of the navy . . . to capture or destroy the garrison there; and . . . with the aid of the navy capture or destroy the Spanish fleet now reported to be in Santiago harbor. . . . On completion of this enterprise, unless you receive other orders or deem it advisable to remain in the harbor of Santiago de Cuba, re-embark your troops and proceed to the harbor of Port de Banes. . . . When will you sail?"

General Shafter could not say, for the orders caught him utterly unprepared—less through his own fault than that of the War Department. Somehow it seemed to expect that Shafter could load his regiments aboard the transports and be off in a matter of a day or so.

Shafter did have transports at Tampa, but not much else. A strange array of vessels chartered by the War Department had begun arriving in April, and one by one the army had refitted most of them with bunks for soldiers and stalls for horses and mules. It was not until June 1, four days after Shafter had received his first order, that they were even ready to take on supplies. The commissary received orders to load six months' rations for twenty thousand men, but had to cut this back to two months' rations. The loading of the guns, caissons, and wagons of the light artillery began, hampered by a search through freight cars for breech mechanisms, and for fuses for the projectiles.

The trouble was only beginning. The loading had to funnel through a tight bottleneck. The promoter, Morton F. Plant, had built Port Tampa only to accommodate small steamers bound for Key West or Cuba. He had dredged a narrow channel along a tongue of land that served as a pier. Only two vessels at a time could stand by it while six other vessels in the channel awaited their turn to load. The army hastily laid additional railroad tracks onto the pier, but most of the loading still had to be done by stevedores who had to carry provisions on their backs from the freight cars across fifty feet of sand and up a steep ramp into the vessels. They were so exhausted that at the completion of their shifts they often slept here and there on the pier.

From the port stretched an even worse obstacle nine miles back to Tampa, the single track of railroad. Plant, who could not subordinate his promoter instincts to the exigencies of war, made it even more unusable by running excursion trains of sightseers in addition to regular train and boat services in and out of Port Tampa during the loading.

The logistics snarl was too complicated for General Shafter to unravel, and although he held conferences day and night, it seemed equally to baffle his subordinates. General Fitzhugh Lee, in charge of the Seventh Corps of volunteers, seemed to have inherited little of his uncle's military genius. As for Shafter, he remained optimistic in the face of chaos and reported May 31 that he thought he could sail in three days. Three days later, General Miles arrived and reported the wildest confusion:

"There are over 300 cars loaded with war material along the roads about Tampa. Stores are sent to the quartermaster at Tampa, but the invoices and bills of lading have not been received, so that officers are obliged to break open seals and hunt from car to car to ascertain whether they contain clothing, grain, balloon material, horse equipments, ammunition, siege guns, commissary stores, etc."

Secretary Alger impatiently replied:

"Twenty thousand men ought to unload any number of cars and assort contents. There is much criticism about delay of expedition. Better leave a fast ship to bring balance material needed than delay longer."

In the end, General Shafter was able to speed the loading by himself supervising, first from the piazza of the Tampa Bay Hotel, and then from the pier at Port Tampa, where a packing case served as a desk and two cracker boxes supported his huge bulk.

General Shafter's corpulence was not only an extreme handicap in the tropical heat, but was a conspicuous target for the gibes of the correspondents. His record for bravery in the Civil War and his long years since as colonel of a regiment patrolling Indians in the West, or on garrison duty at the San Francisco Presidio, did little to prepare him to organize an expedition. But he possessed, as Captain French E. Chadwick of the navy pointed out, "thorough courage, strong will, and much strength of character."

As befitted an old frontier fighter, Shafter was, to the distaste of some correspondents, rather rough in manner and bearing. His years in the West led him to rely upon the regulars, who made up the main body of his expedition, and to trust the regimental commanders to demonstrate initiative in getting men aboard the transports—and later in operations in Cuba.

The colonels justified Shafter's trust. By the time word reached them on June 6 that they should board transports, they had learned that the ships could hold only eighteen thousand or twenty thousand men rather than the anticipated twenty-five thousand. Every regiment engaged in a determined scramble to get aboard, for fear that otherwise it would be left.

Regiment after regiment raced to strike its tents, police camp—burn rubbish and shovel dirt into the "sinks"—and make ready to leave. Trooper Arthur Fortunatus Cosby of the Rough Riders wrote home: "At six o'clock [in the evening] we lined up, the whole regiment, and took the sandy, dirty, hot walk to the Tampa Bay Hotel to be paid off. It was ten by the time we returned, all this for $2.10, my pay. Then we were ordered to prepare at once to leave. We rolled up a sleeping blanket, half of a shelter tent, and poncho with such clothes & comforts as we could, together; threw this over our shoulder, put on our cartridge belts with 125 rounds, took our canteen & eating things, then added a haver-sack (two canvas bags) with some rations issued to us; and with our carbines we were ready."

Then followed a grueling night, for, as Colonel Roosevelt later testified, "there was a good deal of higglety-pigglety business." He jotted in his diary the next day: "Worst confusion yet. R.R. system is utterly mismanaged. No military at head. No allotment of transports. No plans." Some regiments found trains; others did not, but it made little difference since none of them was moving anyway. Every train was trying at the same time to move into Port Tampa on the same single track, with no other way out. Between ten at night and daybreak, the track was so congested that no troops reached the pier at all.

The Rough Riders, Cosby wrote, "marched first to one place, then another. Finally about midnight we reached a place on the railroad where the command was given 'At rest.'

"About five we had the usual experience of 'rustling' for coffee and did the best we could. Then we were put on coal freight cars and rode to Port Tampa in about an hour. We were afraid that we should have to foot it, and were only too delighted to get a lift."

Many regiments had to move to the port in freight cars, and some fared worse than the Rough Riders. William Dinwiddie reported in the Washington *Star:* "One regiment:—the 6th U.S. Infantry—struck its tents at 9 o'clock Tuesday night, and waited until 2 o'clock Wednesday at Tampa before it was moved. The experience of these men was particularly discouraging since they traveled in a stock train, standing for four hours in soft filth, while the cars were side-tracked and jostled about in the scalding midday sun. Hardly a murmur came from the men when they were put aboard this ill-smelling train, so great was the desire of every man to go to the front."

At the pier, the tired and hungry men often had to stand for hours before they were put aboard transports. The Negro troops of the Tenth Cavalry under Captain John Bigelow, Jr., traveled to the pier in railroad coaches that even had ice in the water coolers, but had nothing to eat after a 3 A.M. breakfast of coffee and hardtack. "I wanted to give my men some supper," Bigelow wrote. "I went to a restaurant on the pier to make arrangements to have the men eat there, and was told by the lady who kept it that to have colored men eat in her dining-room would ruin her business." Except for what they could purchase from peddlers, they had to sleep unfed, and the next morning load baggage, still without rations.

Even the correspondents and artists suffered relative hardships. Some eighty-nine of them, mostly staying at the Tampa Bay Hotel, received word on the night of June 7 to board the headquarters ship, the *Segurança,* or other of the transports, at two in the morning. "The excitement which followed was tremendous," Dinwiddie reported. "For the next few hours the corridors and lobbies were jammed with men and luggage. . . . It was a motley assembly which scurried through the hotel, in canvas hunting suits, in white ducks, in the brown fatigue clothes of the army, and even in immaculate white shirt fronts and patent leathers. Six-shooters, machetes and belts full of ammunition circulated through the halls, while broad shoulders were strung with shoulder straps from which dangled canteens, rolls of blankets, binoculars, kodaks and pouches filled with notebooks. . . .

"Two o'clock came, and then 3, and 4 and 5, bringing the first glimmer of a beautiful dawn, before the train was loaded with headquarters' and correspondents' luggage and pulled slowly away from the great hostelry, where, so far as outsiders could see, had been enacted one long comedy of gaiety and pleasure for seven weeks."

When the correspondents arrived at the docks on the morning of Wednesday, June 8, they reported scenes of excited disorder. As the troops stood around the transports that hectic day, there was little military display. "There was no martial music," reported Dinwiddie, "nor the orderly and steady tramp, tramp of the flower of the army, as described by some of our more impressionable and poetic writers, but in their place was the grim determination of every commanding officer, every overworked quartermaster, to get his regiment on board some particular transport. The docks were piled high with tentage, luggage and commissary supplies, and the sweltering, already-tired soldiery struggled in long, thin, loaded lines, to get their stuff aboard. It was a wonderful spectacular performance, one to be seen, not described."

It was the sort in which men like Colonel Roosevelt were most effective. He later testified that when his men reached Port Tampa early in the morning:

"There were a lot of regiments there; the trains backed up everywhere along the quay, and the quay was swarming with some 10,000 men—soldiers, mostly. . . . The quartermaster, Colonel Humphrey . . . allotted us the *Yucatan*. . . . Colonel Wood jumped in a boat and went out in midstream [to commandeer it]. I happened to find out by accident that the transport *Yucatan* had also been allotted to the Second Infantry and the Seventy-first New York, and I ran down to my men and left a guard and took the rest and rushed them down to the dock

and got on the *Yucatan,* holding the gangplank against the
Second Infantry and Seventy-first New York."

Lieutenant William Rockwell of the Seventy-first remembered that when Captain Anthony J. Bleecker went to capture
the *Yucatan,* this interchange took place:

"Hello," said Roosevelt, "what can I do for you?"

"That's our ship," said Bleecker.

"Well, we seem to have it," replied the smiling Roosevelt.

In testifying, Roosevelt wound up with a flourish: "I understand the Seventy-first spent the next two nights on a train. We
ultimately kept four companies of the Second Infantry aboard
with us, but we had the *Yucatan.*" He failed to add that after several hours, the rival Seventy-first had marched smartly aboard a
newer and more comfortable ship, the *Vigilancia.*

In this fashion, the army loaded the largest military expedition which had ever left the United States. The transports carried
819 officers, 15,058 enlisted men, 30 civilian clerks, 272 team-
sters and packers, and 107 stevedores. There were 2,295 horses
and mules with harness, 114 six-mule army wagons, and 81 escort
wagons—but only 7 ambulances, since it was thought that army
wagons could serve the purpose. Two additional pack trains and
then ambulances were sent later. The artillery consisted of sixteen
light guns, four 7-inch howitzers, four 5-inch siege guns, one
Hotchkiss revolving cannon, one pneumatic dynamite gun, eight
3.6-inch field mortars, and four Gatling machine guns.

At the close of this spectacle came a surprising denouement.
About two in the afternoon, when the ships were finally loaded
and heading down the bay, the exhausted Shafter, on his way to
board the headquarters ship, received a wire from Secretary
Alger: "Wait until you get further orders before you sail."
Without comment, Shafter called back the ships that had started, and went aboard the *Segurança.*

The reason for the delay was a report by the converted
yacht *Eagle* the previous evening that it had sighted a Spanish

armored cruiser second class and a torpedo-boat destroyer in the San Nicolás Channel. The *Resolute* confirmed this. Thus for days while the navy tried to run down these two nonexistent Spanish vessels—the "Phantom Fleet," the army sneered—the expedition sat sweltering aboard the transports in Tampa Bay.

For the troops, correspondents, and spectators, it was a sad anticlimax. Wrote Dinwiddie of the frustrating afternoon of June 8:

"This fearful activity, this stupendous energy evidenced by an army suddenly electrified into motion was all for naught and for nearly five whole days the army lay idly at rest, waiting patiently. . . . It was a frightful ordeal for the army . . . one in which the men suffered mental depression and physical devitalization, largely shared by the ranking officers, who feared that, under the torrid suns and in the superheated and illy-ventilated holds, where the masses of the army lay gasping, an outbreak of fever was imminent. Fevers did appear, but fortunately they were all malarial, and the dread typhus did not make its appearance."

Roosevelt wrote angrily that the soldiers were "jammed together under the tropical sun on these crowded troop ships. We are in a sewer; a canal which is festering as if it were Havana harbor."

The delay was a godsend to Shafter, who used the time to continue the sorting and loading of essential equipment. Indeed, when orders to sail came on June 12, medical supplies had just arrived. Even then it took two days to reload animals and replenish the water on the transports.

These were nervous as well as unpleasant days for the soldiers. Trooper Cosby, like many another, had gone to the photographer in Tampa to have his picture taken, and wondered vaguely if it might be his last. It was a perfect likeness, he wrote his mother, and the strange costume, the brown canvas fatigue uniform of the cavalry, was exactly what the Rough Riders were wearing. They were fortunate not to be sweltering in woolens like the regulars.

When the flotilla steamed out of Tampa Bay on June 14 after so many weary postponements and delays, Richard Harding Davis wrote that both the troops on the ships and the spectators ashore were suspicious and wary. From the transports there was no waving, yelling, or bandplaying, and on the docks there were only "three colored women and a pathetic group of perspiring stevedores and three soldiers" to wave farewells.

Outside of Tampa Bay the vessels formed three long lines: thirty-two transports, one of them towing a barge and another a schooner carrying water—a folly, as Roosevelt called it, which cut the speed of the convoy to a scow's pace. There were also three lighters, one of which sank en route. Surrounding these was an array of protecting naval vessels. The navy suggested breaking the transports of protecting naval vessels into two divisions and sending the swifter part ahead, but Shafter refused. He did agree to try to run the convoy at the speed of the slowest vessels, but he abandoned this after they had gone halfway and the ships were spread out for thirty or forty miles.

"We traveled at the rate of seven miles an hour, with long pauses for thought and consultation," Davis reported. "Sometimes we moved at the rate of four miles an hour, and frequently we did not move at all." Consequently the trip from Tampa to Santiago, Cuba, took five and a half days. The expedition "moved through a succession of sparkling, sunlit days, over a sea as smooth as a lake, undisturbed by Spanish cruisers or by shells from Spanish forts. As far as the eye could see it had the ocean entirely to itself."

The convoying naval vessels, headed by the *Indiana*, impressed Davis. He wrote: "The war-ships treated us with the most punctilious courtesy and concealed contempt. And we certainly deserved it. We could not keep in line and we lost ourselves and each other, and the gun-boats and torpedo-boats were busy rounding us up, and giving us sharp, precise orders in passing, through a megaphone, to which either nobody on board made any reply, or everyone did. The gun-boats were like swift, keen-eyed, intelligent collies rounding up a herd of bungling sheep. They looked so workmanlike and clean, and the men were so smart in their white duck, that the soldiers cheered them all along the line, as they dashed up and down it, waving their wig-wags frantically."

As the convoy circled north of Cuba, it dawdled for days alone the shore, a barely moving target for the Spaniards. General Wheeler noted in his diary on June 17: "At 10 o'clock we are passing the Cuban lighthouse at Paradone Principe. We can plainly see the barracks that are occupied by Spanish soldiers, and some contend they can see the men standing in front of the buildings." At night, the Spaniards at least turned off the lights in the Cuban lighthouses, but not so with the Americans. The running lights of the convoy appeared to Charles M. Pepper of the Washington *Star* "like the struggling street of a floating city. . . . The signals were flashed at a lively rate for a time like a string of colored lanterns swinging from the masts." Other lights were out aboard the transports, except for Shafter's headquarters ship, which sailed brightly lit from stem to stern, with a band loudly playing ragtime. Altogether, the flotilla was as conspicuous, wrote Davis, as "Brooklyn or New York, with the lights of the bridge included."

Some of the nervous military and naval attachés aboard recalled French maneuvers they had witnessed in which the torpedo squadron had in theory massacred much of the fleet. Their talk drifted to the possibility that Spanish torpedo boats might come darting out from the shore to sink transport as they straggled along in the darkness, or passed through the Bahama Channel, which for a distance of twelve miles was only seven miles wide.

"The foreign attachés," wrote Davis, "regarded the fair weather that accompanied us, the brutal good health of the men, the small loss of horses and mules, and the entire freedom from interference on the part of the enemy with the same grudging envy that one watches a successful novice winning continuously at roulette. . . .

"It was a most happy-go-lucky expedition, run with real American optimism and readiness to take big chances, and with the spirit of a people who recklessly trust that it will come out all right in the end, and that the barely possible may not happen. . . . As one of the generals on board said, 'This is God Almighty's war, and we are only His agents.'"

The enlisted men floated along with few of these worries and a comparatively cheerful attitude. They complained little about the real hardship of their ten or twelve days on a transport: serious overcrowding, dark makeshift quarters in the holds, tasteless cold food, and nauseous warm water. Rough Rider Cosby, used to comfortable living, took it as part of the adventure:

"My troop was given quarters in the second lower deck, in the hold where coal has evidently been carried. Tiers of 3 bunks were made and there we lie. I have been lucky enough to get a bit of the upper deck where I spread my blanket and sleep in comfort. The men lie so close together that you cannot walk. Below deck where the freight portholes are opened there is a fair breeze and the men sleep comfortably."

On the deck, Cosby would lie at night on his blanket, using his shoes as a pillow. "The sentry passes by, men step on you and over you, but somehow you sleep on."

"Personally I expected anything and I have no complaints to make," Cosby wrote a friend, "but a lot of the 'boys' don't like it. Our food on board ship is the same; coffee, hardtack, with canned beef (that must have been cooked it is so stringy and tasteless), canned tomatoes and beans. These are travel rations and we have now had 10 days of them with 5 days more on the road. We get the coffee hot, but the other things are usually cold unless an enterprising fellow will make a mess of the whole thing which he calls a stew.

"We have all gone expert in 'rustling' food, begging it, buying it from the ship's cook who is supposed not to sell, smuggling it in from shore etc. As my troop K is enterprising we fare quite well. . . .

"All the boys have lost flesh at the most astonishing rate. . . . Then too although our passage has been remarkably quiet many of the boys have been sea-sick. This with the confinement and heat to which they are not accustomed, and poor food has weakened them. I am very much afraid that we shan't do much."

At daybreak on Monday, June 20, they sighted the rugged mountains of the Sierra Maestra wrapped in a blue mist. They reminded the men from the West of the mountains of Arizona. The troops made up their rolls, preparatory to disembarking, and crowded the rails in anticipation. Within a few hours they sighted through the haze the Morro Castle of Santiago and the semicircle of the blockading fleet surrounding the harbor entrance.

While the convoy waited, Admiral Sampson came aboard the *Segurança* to sail with General Shafter eighteen miles west of Santiago to confer ashore with the Cuban General Calixto García, who could give them detailed information about the Spanish land forces. As the navy gig pulled up onto a beach overhung with palms, a double line of Cuban officers stood drawn up in their honor. Stripped Cuban soldiers, shouting and cheering, rushed into the water to haul the boats ashore or to carry some of the officers and correspondents on their shoulders. A mile inland, General Calixto García met them. He was impressive with his white mustache and goatee and the deep bullet scar in his forehead where he had tried to kill himself ten years before when he was a captive of the Spaniards.

In a palm-frond hut, they held a council of war. Admiral Sampson wanted the army to land at both sides of the entrance to Santiago harbor and charge up the steep slopes to capture Morro Castle and the sister batteries at Socapa. Then the navy would sweep the mines from the harbor entrance and attack the Spanish fleet. Shafter, who on his way to Cuba had been reading an account of a disastrous eighteenth-century British expedition against Santiago, had come to his own conclusions. He wished no such bloody undertaking as would be involved in storming a stone fort perched on a 230-foot cliff. He wrote later: "It would have been the height of folly." Neither did he wish to imitate the British, who had succumbed to yellow fever trying to fight their way from Guantánamo, an excellent harbor but forty miles east.

Instead, Shafter followed his own previous inclination, in which the Cubans concurred. He decided to land at Daiquiri, fifteen miles east of Santiago, and at Siboney nearby, even though this would involve disembarking from an open roadstead onto beaches where prevailing winds piled a heavy swell every afternoon. The Cubans told him that there were only three hundred Spanish troops at Daiquiri. They promised their cooperation in driving them away and making feints elsewhere to distract the Spanish when the Americans came ashore.

Before dawn on Wednesday, June 22, Trooper Cosby hastily wrote his mother: "The orders are to land this morning at daybreak. It is scarcely that yet. . . . Only eight of the transports are to land this morning. We are one of them. We were up at 4 o'clock. One day's rations have been issued to us, and all are packed ready to land. It will be a welcome change from this ship-board life. Fifteen days is rather tiresome.

"I do not think we shall have any fighting where we are going to land but there is always the chance. I have often wondered how it felt to be on the eve of a battle but it is no different from anything else.

"The sun is rising and we are drawing nearer shore so goodbye."

6

Daiquiri Beachhead

If the Spanish army had displayed even moderate initiative, it could have turned the landing at Daiquiri into one of the most costly and painful military disasters in United States history. Lieutenant General Arsenio Linares Pombo was well aware that the American forces would undoubtedly try to land either to the west of Santiago harbor near Punta Cabrera or, more likely, to the east at Daiquiri and Siboney. Both were highly defensible beaches, for wherever the Americans tried to land they would have to anchor in relatively open roadstead and come ashore through heavy surf. Behind the beach for twenty miles on each side of Santiago was a commanding limestone bluff, at most points 200 to 250 feet high. At key locations along this ridge and on strategic hilltops inland, the Spanish had built blockhouses which were particularly effective defenses against either invading forces or insurgents.

Against strong fortifications in rugged terrain, and against twelve thousand seasoned Spanish soldiers, General Shafter prepared to land his expedition of seventeen thousand men. He wisely chose to establish a beachhead at the spot from which he could most easily storm Santiago; the western approaches were too close to Spanish naval guns and strong army units. Yet had General Linares chosen to leave only a thin line of interior defense against the ineffective Cubans and to align his troops and artillery in the blockhouses and along the ridges behind Daiquiri, Siboney, and the beaches west of Santiago, he scarcely could have failed to hurl back the American invaders with disastrous losses. The United States Navy bombardment could scarcely have pinpointed the Spanish positions, and troops could not have landed in the face of fire as heavy and accurate as they later faced at the edge of Santiago. This was why the foreign attachés were predicting disaster to General Shafter. "They talked to me most consolingly," he later recalled.

Shafter was not so foolhardy as to attempt a landing against determined opposition. He had learned from the Cubans that only a handful of Spaniards were defending Daiquiri; a Cuban regiment had promised to drive them out. With considerable optimism, therefore, he told his command, his adjutant general, E. J. McClernand, remembered, "that we were a long way from the Civil War; that the country was no longer accustomed to hear of heavy losses in battle and would judge us accordingly; that he intended to get his army in position around the city of Santiago and demand a surrender."

One other thing was clear to Shafter from his reading of British disasters and his own earlier experience with yellow fever: "There is no more use in thinking that men can go into that climate at that season of the year and escape distress, than there is that you can put your hand in the fire and escape burning. . . . I determined to rush it, and I did rush it."

Realistically, with more fear of the fever than of the Spanish, General Shafter prepared to land his forces on the morning of June 22. Nevertheless, it was a nervous night, for before dawn, fires broke out ashore. Were the Spaniards signaling and planning a sturdy defense after all? With daylight, the soldiers gazed expectantly at the apparently deserted hamlet where they were to land. The high iron pier the Spanish American Iron Company used for the loading of ore loomed forty feet or more above the water. On it, an ore car was ablaze, and ashore the company's machine shop was also on fire. There was no other sign that people were around, but ominously atop a steep knob commanding the town and the roadstead was a Spanish blockhouse.

By nine o'clock, heavily laden troops had clambered down into small boats preparatory to landing. Then, as they bobbed in the water, they could hear naval vessels stretched along twenty miles of coast opening a bombardment; transports west of Santiago feinted a landing. Six ships, the *New Orleans, Vixen, Wasp, Hornet,* and *Scorpion,* opened fire on Daiquiri. Kennett F. Harris of the Chicago *Record* wrote: "At first we experienced a thrill of excitement, a fullness at the throat and a quick, cold touch upon the vertebral nerve centers when the white smoke burst from the sides of the vessels, one following another; and we cheered madly, not knowing exactly why."

"For twenty minutes," reported Malcolm McDowell of the *Record,* "the rapid-firing and machine guns beat the long roll with the heavy ones coming in with booms and thumps like a great bass drum. The shells ripped through the trees, smashed the cliffs, uprooted great palms and tore up the earth with a vindictive vigor which delighted the soldiers." But not a shot hit the Spanish blockhouse.

No return fire came from the blockhouse or elsewhere on shore. Indeed, the bombardment seemed destructive only of the hillside and several of the waiting Cuban allies. A solitary

Cuban appeared at the end of the iron pier, energetically waving a white cloth to signal that the Spaniards were gone.

It signaled as well the beginning of a helter-skelter disembarkation. Persuading the cautious captains of the transports to
bring their vessels close enough to shore to unload troops was
no easy task. Many took their ships miles out to sea and ignored
orders. Lieutenant Colonel Roosevelt, through a combination
of luck and enterprise, did better with the *Yucatan:*

"My former naval aide, while I was Assistant Secretary of the
Navy, Lieutenant Sharp, was in command of the *Vixen*, a converted yacht; and everything being managed on the go-as-you-
please principle, he steamed by us and offered to help put us
ashore. Of course, we jumped at the chance. Wood and I board-
ed the *Vixen*, and there we got Lieutenant Sharp's black Cuban
pilot, who told us he could take our transport right in to within
a few hundred yards of the land. Accordingly, we put him
aboard; and in he brought her, gaining at least a mile and a half
by the manoeuvre. The other transports followed; but we had
our berth, and were all right."

Only the example of the *Yucatan*, together with "an intensive
airing of the opinions of many," persuaded the captain of the
Matteawan to move slowly inshore. The most stubborn of the
skippers was that of the *San Marcos*, who did not land his men
for another two days. When the captain was ordered to bring
his ship close to the Siboney beach, according to the recollec-
tion of B. T. Simmons of the Sixteenth Infantry, "he started
towards shore, became afraid and ran toward El Morro until he
was turned back by a ship of the blockading squadron. When
he repeated this, General Shafter followed us, and, through a
megaphone, gave the master a characteristic and artistic 'cussing
out.'" But even General Shatter couldn't curse the ship really
close to shore.

Others had begun to unload soldiers as the last echoes of
the bombardment died away on the morning of June 22. "Under

the cover of the smoke," wrote Richard Harding Davis, "the long-boats and launches began to scurry toward the shore. . . . The men in the boats pulled harder at the oars, the steam-launches rolled and pitched, tugging at the weight behind them [as they towed the lines of boats], and the first convoy of five hundred men were soon bunched together, racing bow by bow for the shore. A launch turned suddenly and steered for a long pier under the ore-docks, the waves lifted it to the level of the pier, and a half-dozen men leaped through the air and landed on the pier-head, waving their muskets above them. At the same moment two of the other boats were driven through the surf to the beach itself, and the men tumbled out and scrambled to their feet upon the shore of Cuba. In an instant a cheer rose faintly from the shore, and more loudly from the war-ships. It was caught up by every ship in the transport fleet, and was carried for miles over the ocean. Men waved their hats, and jumped up and down, and shrieked as though they themselves had been the first to land."

It was a tense moment for the correspondents and foreign attachés, all of whom were still on shipboard. As the troops headed ashore in the overhanging smoke, Frederic Remington reported: "We held our breath. We expected a most desperate fight for the landing." It was with great relief that they saw the distant tiny figures rush up the beach. It was also with intense irritation over General Shafter's orders, holding them on the ships until after the troops had landed. While the boats were being assembled, an acid interchange took place on the promenade deck of the *Segurança* between General Shafter and Richard Harding Davis. Shafter's adjutant general remembered years later:

"Mr. Davis said: 'General, I see the order for disembarkation . . . will keep back reporters.' He was told that was true, but it [indicated] . . . only a desire to be prepared as far as possible to return the fire of the Spaniards in the event that some of them still remained in the woods back of the beach. . . .

"Finally, Mr. Davis said he was not an ordinary reporter, but a descriptive writer. At this the General's patience, never very long, gave way and he replied in a sharp tone: 'I do not care a damn what you are. I'll treat all of you alike.' Mr. Davis was offended at the abruptness of the reply and never afterwards, so far as I know, said a kindly word about General Shafter."

So was many another correspondent, for few of them grasped the potential seriousness of the landing. Even Burr McIntosh, who did realize it, commented a few months later: "From the moment of the issuing of that order, pencils began to be sharpened for General Shafter—and they have not yet lost their point." McIntosh tried to slip into one of the longboats leaving the *Matteawan*, but the captains of each company were watching them closely as they loaded. He rolled up a bundle of clothing and a camera for an orderly to take ashore, dropped over the side, and tried swimming in against a strong riptide. Part of the way he clung to one of the towlines pulling the boats, so soon he was ashore taking pictures.

Landing by boat through the heavy surf or bobbing next to the pier was dangerous enough. "There was the jam of craft at the jetty," reported Harris, "[and] the momentary expectation of being smashed like egg shells against the slimy piles." In the afternoon, two Negro soldiers, Corporal Cobb and Private English, of the Tenth Cavalry, slipped while climbing from the lighter to the pier. One of the Rough Riders, Captain Bucky O'Neill, mayor of Prescott, Arizona, plunged fully clothed into the water after them, but the men were crushed before he could reach them. Several boats and one of the launches capsized or were smashed by the heavy seas, but these were the only casualties.

Although Siboney, miles nearer to Santiago, was clear for landing the next day, the artillery slowly disembarked on June 23 and 24 at Daiquiri. One of the artillery officers, F. S. Hodgson, remembered:

"The guns and ammunition [were] lightered ashore to the
... dock of the ... Iron Company, while the horses were
unloaded by throwing them overboard where they were caught
up by the ship's boats, led to the breakers by their halter shanks
and turned loose to be washed ashore or received by a detachment on the beach. A few of the bolder spirits among the landing detachments attached a heaving line to their waists and
went through the heavy surf to receive the animals and were
then drawn through the breakers by others on the shore, dangerous work but exciting sport.

"In spite of the conditions, the horses were disembarked
with comparatively small loss, but were almost unfit for any
kind of service for an extended period as a result of their confinement in the hot, dark hold of the transport. They were a
sorry looking lot as they stood on the picket lines, the picture
of dejection and weariness."

No more than fifty horses died on the long, sweltering trip,
and only five or six drowned coming ashore, which was remarkable in those rough waters. When a group of cavalry horses
began to swim to sea, a bugler ashore blew the proper call; they
wheeled around and headed for the shore.

During that first day, despite the disorganized nature of the
landing, six thousand troops came ashore. It seemed almost
miraculous that they were able to do so without a single Spanish
shot being fired against them. They found eight thousand
rounds of Mauser rifle ammunition left behind, and many official papers in the house of the commandant. On the desk was
an unfinished letter in which he begged "to assure his excellen-
cy [General Linares] that he was abundantly able to resist any
attack at Daiquiri, either by land or sea." The ammunition, and
rifle pits running in every direction, convinced the tacticians of
the Fifth Corps that the commandant had been correct. Linares
had pulled him back toward Santiago.

When General Wheeler came ashore, he sent several Rough Riders to run up the United States flag over the unscathed blockhouse. The sight of it produced wild jubilation among the nervous soldiers. Malcolm McDowell wrote: "A quarter of an hour of whistle shrieks, cheers, yells, drum flares, bugle calls and patriotic songs were sent up. . . . Then the noise ceased, and out of it came the strains of the 'Star Spangled Banner' from the regimemental band on the *Matteawan*. The soldiers ashore and the soldiers afloat were quiet until the brasses became silent, and then three full-lunged hurrahs crashed against the hill, and the salute to the flag was complete."

"A little later," reported Kennett F. Harris, "with Capt. O'Neill, I climbed the hill to the still smoking ruins of the roundhouse that the Spanish had burned before evacuating the town. There were a few charred timbers still standing over the mass of twisted bolts, shafts and plates that had been a loco-motive. Farther back was an armored car in good condition, and all about were heaps of exploded cartridges that had been thrown into the flames."

In Siboney the next day, Orrin R. Wolfe of the Twenty-sec-ond Infantry found about half a dozen locomotives in a round-house. The Spanish had tried to sabotage them by destroying a vital part, such as a driving rod, from each of them. "I knew I had a number of men in the company who had been railroad men," Wolfe reminisced. "We worked for some time, taking a part from one engine and putting it in the place of a part that was missing. One was ready to go about 3:00 P.M. We only had a little water, but a water tank was about 200 yards down the road, so we had up steam. I was in the cab with three or four sol-diers, one acting as engineer. I got hold of the whistle cord and proceeded to toot. We ran out of round-house and down the track, soldiers cheering."

The railroad tracks were so damaged that the locomotives could not haul troops, supplies, or artillery from Daiquiri; for

Boatload of Rough Riders leaving the Yucatan

Men climbing onto the dock at Daiquiri

Troops moving toward the interior, Daiquiri

this the army had to depend upon a narrow, almost impassable road.

"They say the first man who landed inquired the way to Santiago," General Shafter boasted afterward. "I don't know whethere he did or not, but the first organized command which reached shore took the road to Santiago, and didn't stop until they got there." This in essence was the history of the first week after the initial landing. Even with the aid of the navy it went slowly—as slowly as the embarkation—and this alone delayed the forward motion of the troops. About four on the first afternoon, General Shafter ordered General H. W. Lawton to march with two regiments to occupy Siboney, which the Spaniards had also abandoned during the naval bombardment. At nightfall, he was only partway and camped on the road. The troops were bivouacked from Daiquiri along four or five miles of road.

The soldiers were fearful during their first night on the Cuban coast—they were so vulnerable to surprise attack from the Spanish forces. More than once, sentries, hearing a rustling nearby, fired, only to find the intruders were the fearful-looking but harmless land crabs. They almost defeated the Sixth Infantry that first night, Edward R. Chrisman reminisced. "The fight lasted all night long and [they] almost drove us from our position, outnumbered as we were dozens to one in the darkness and ceaseless rain. . . . To be awakened from a doze of exhaustion by soaking rain, with land crabs clinging to one's ears, nose and hands and creeping all over the body, is not soothing to the nerves of those accustomed to the ways of this scavenger."

The land crabs were so hateful to the soldiers that they paid less attention to that other nuisance, swarms of mosquitoes. Nor did they know that these were their deadliest enemies in Cuba, the carriers of yellow fever.

Drenched, bitten by mosquitoes, but still in good health, the troops marched on into Siboney the morning after the first landing, June 23, 1898. It immediately became the main American base for the assault upon Santiago. Shafter transferred most of the unloading of men and supplies there. What had been a hamlet of no more than a thousand people became the headquarters for ordnance, the quartermaster, commissary, and medical corps. One of the newspapermen, H. Irving Hancock, wrote:

"Near the beach was a cluster of a dozen or so of squalid houses, in the midst of which towered a sawmill and a storehouse. The former was promptly taken possession of by the engineers; the latter was just the kind of building to suit the commissary. West of these buildings flowed a sluggish creek, emptying into a stagnant pond, which, though it had no outlet, was separated from the ocean by only a few yards of sandy beach. All around this creek were swamp and slime—an ideal soil for breeding malaria and fever germs." It was days before the engineers found time to cut through the sandbar to let the ocean into the brackish pond. Siboney was already infested with yellow fever; some of the victims and quantities of other Cuban refugees and soldiers filled the town when the Americans arrived.

The romantic American troops had greeted the first Cuban soldiers with hearty cheers they landed at Daiquiri. "Viva Cuba libre," they had yelled. "Vivan los Americanos," the Cubans had shouted back. These were the heroes they had come to rescue, who for so long had been harassing the Spaniards. And indeed it was the Cubans who fought a skirmish against the retreating Spanish rear guard as the Americans advanced from Daiquiri to Siboney. The Americans thought that, given rations, arms, and ammunition, the Cuban troops would fight bravely and be of great aid.

"The day of the landing at Daiquiri, Castillo's regiment from Bayamo was coming through," Charles M. Pepper wrote in the Washington Star. "The strings of cloth which answered for shirts and other garments could hardly be said to clothe the nakedness of the men. Some were barefoot, while others had a kind of straw sandal, which protected the sole of the foot. A few had machetes alone, but the majority had guns as well. These were the old style Remingtons or discarded Springfields. The regiments of General Calixto García's command, which were subsequently landed at Siboney, were no better clad. . . . They waded through the surf clutching their guns as a possession infinitely more valuable than clothes."

What were the military potentialities of these men, Hancock asked a foreign correspondent who was also an army major. "'Well,' replied the Major, with a quizzical smile, 'I guess they'll fight. I don't quite see how such ragged fellows can, with modesty, turn their back upon the enemy.'"

The sympathetic Americans readily shared their rations with both soldiers and civilian refugees. "Whenever one lighted a fire a Cuban presented himself, at the sign of the smoke, quietly and inexplicably like a genie, and asked for food," wrote John Black Atkins of the Manchester *Guardian*. "Some of the insurgents assumed quite a different appearance by garnishing the 'loop'd and window'd raggedness' with parts of the United States uniform. The roads about Siboney might have been the scene of a stampede, so littered were they with pieces of soldiers' equipments," discarded in the heat of the march.

And so it was, as Atkins pointed out, that even before they had met the Spanish oppressors, the American troops became disgusted with the Cubans they had come to liberate:

"At once they became 'tired,' because the Cuban insurgent regarded every American as a kind of charitable institution, and expected him to disgorge on every occasion. The Cuban was continually pointing to the American's shirt, coat, or trousers, and then pointing to himself, meaning that he desired a transfer of property.

"Then other things outraged the feeling of the American soldiers—the cruelty of Cubans, for example. One day a bull was found in Siboney, and was to be killed for food. The American soldiers wished to shoot it, but the Cubans would not have a bull killed in that way. The creature was stabbed and stabbed with their knives till it fell, and the incident sank more deeply than one would have supposed into the minds of the soldiers. . . .

"'Why,' [the Americans] asked in effect, 'should we fight for men like these? They are no better than the Spaniards.' And it escaped the notice of nearly all, that mean and savage ways were to be expected in those who had long been treated with meanness and savagery."

Late into the second night, American troops poured ashore at Siboney, no more than three miles from the Spanish outposts. Richard Harding Davis reported the scene with wonder:

"No one slept that night, for until two o'clock in the morning troops were still being disembarked in the surf, and two ships of war had their searchlights turned on the landing-place, and made Siboney as light as a ball-room. Back of the searchlights was an ocean white with moonlight, and on the shore red camp-fires, at which the half-drowned troops were drying their uniforms, and the Rough Riders, who had just marched in from Daiquiri, were cooking their coffee and bacon. Below the former home of the Spanish commandant, which General Wheeler had made his head-quarters, lay the camp of the Rough Riders, and through it Cuban officers were riding their half-starved ponies, scattering the ashes of the camp-fires, and galloping over the tired bodies of the men with that courtly grace and consideration for Americans which invariably marks the Cuban gentleman. Below them was the beach and the roaring surf, in which a thousand or so naked men were assisting and impeding the progress shoreward of their comrades, in pontoons and shore-boats, which were being hurled at the beach like sleds down a water-chute.

"It was one of the most weird and remarkable scenes of the war, probably of any war. An army was being landed on an enemy's coast at the dead of night, but with somewhat more of cheers and shrieks and laughter than rise from the bathers in the surf at Coney Island on a hot Sunday. It was a pandemonium of noises. The men still to be landed from the 'prison hulks,' as they called the transports, were singing in chorus, the men already on shore were dancing naked around the camp-fires on the beach, or shouting with delight as they plunged into the first bath that had offered in seven days, and those in the launches as they were pitched headfirst at the soil of Cuba, signalized their arrival by howls of triumph."

Their noise must have carried faintly to the Spanish troops working hastily that night to strengthen the fortifications at Las Guásimas which guarded the road to Santiago. Had they advanced that night into the black overhanging ridges that rose directly behind Siboney, they could have wrought serious damage to the landing Americans. Instead they waited in their positions, against which General Wheeler intended to march his dismounted cavalry in the morning.

General Joseph Wheeler

General Wheeler, C.S.A., as Brady photographed him

7

Skirmish at Las Guásimas

Early on the morning of June 24, 1898, Major General Joseph Wheeler threw his troops against the Spaniards to dislodge them from strong positions at Las Guásimas. It was the first land battle of the war.

There might have been something comic about the manner in which "Fighting Joe" Wheeler managed to circumvent General Shafter's intention to hold back the dismounted cavalry as a rear guard at Daiquiri. While Shafter was still aboard a transport, Wheeler was the top-ranking officer ashore. Besides, Shafter's orders did not reach him in time.

There was nothing ridiculous about General Wheeler's decision to attack. The Spaniards were uncomfortably close to the beachhead, and they were holding a well-fortified strategic gap in the hills through which the American troops must pass on their way to Santiago. Just beyond the gap was a well-watered plain around Sevilla, the only good site for an American camp between the beach and the fortifications guarding Santiago, and a camp must be established while artillery and supplies were slowly coming to the front. The sooner Wheeler seized Las Guásimas the better. He knew precisely where the enemy were, since General Castillo's Cuban troops had fought a brief encounter against them the day before, and he knew the Spanish forces were relatively few in number. If he was foolhardy, it was only in sending his men along narrow jungle roads and trails where they could easily have been ambushed, carrying with him no artillery with which to shell the enemy fortifications except three Hotchkiss revolving cannons.

The Spaniards should have fought the decisive battle of the war at Las Guásimas, Colonel Herbert H. Sargent of the Fifth United States Volunteer Infantry later argued in his three-volume analysis of the Santiago campaign. From their trenches at the crest of a 250-foot ridge they commanded the rugged terrain, thick with tangled vegetation, that stretched back to the beach. Nor could they be bypassed without leaving the base of supplies at Siboney unprotected. The Spanish could have arrayed their army there without risk to Santiago. Indeed, they would have better protected the city, since they would have guarded the water and food supply lines and the road over which six thousand additional troops should have been rushed from Guantánamo, only forty-two miles away. Had Linares's main army fought at Las Guásimas with the skill and courage it demonstrated later, it could have blocked the American forces on the miasmic coastal strip until yellow fever came to the rescue of the Spaniards. General Wheeler was wise to strike the lightly held fortifications quickly before Linares could change his mind and reinforce them. He did not know until later that Linares had made the incredibly foolish decision to abandon them without a fight. Had Wheeler been a poorer general and slower, there would have been no skirmish at Las Guásimas.

It was a dangerous mission upon which General Wheeler embarked his men that June morning, but it was also a moment of renewed glory. He had been waiting for it for many long years since his career as a dashing Confederate cavalry leader had ended after Appomattox in prison with Jefferson Davis, in the custody of General Nelson A. Miles. His fame as a Confederate general had carried him, a planter-lawyer-politician, into Congress, where for twenty years he had served the new businessmen's South in which the blue and gray had long been reunited. When he arrived at Tampa, an officer inquired, "And how does it feet, General, to wear the blue again?" Wheeler, an old West Pointer, replied, "I feel as though I had been away on a three weeks' furlough and had but just come back to my own colors."

"I go out this morning with Wood's regiment and will press on to Seville," Wheeler notified headquarters on June 24. "Yesterday afternoon I went out three miles toward Santiago. The road is very good."

The road was good only in comparison with part of that linking Daiquiri with Siboney. Wheeler ordered General S. B. M. Young's brigade of the First and Tenth (Negro) Regular Cavalry out along it. At the same time Colonel Wood's First Volunteer Cavalry were to make their way along a steep and difficult trail paralleling the road to the left. The two units would converge at Las Guásimas. General Castillo's Cuban forces of about eight hundred men were to accompany them.

At 5:45 in the morning, Young's right column began its advance; Wood's troops started up the hillside behind Siboney fifteen minutes later. Guards refused to allow the Americans to awaken General Castillo; he and his troops slept on. Most of the correspondents accompanied the Rough Riders. Kennett F. Harris of the Chicago *Record* wrote:

"Col. Wood jumped up and snapped his watch shut. 'We start in five minutes,' he said. 'Any one who isn't ready will be left behind. . . .' Troop L was in advance, and as I stopped to fill my canteen I caught sight of Capt. Capron's tall figure striding over the boulders in the steep ascent and stopping now and then to beckon his men on. . . .

"It was a hard hill to climb, and there were frequent halts. Two companies of the 22d Infantry had started for the crest five minutes before to relieve their pickets, who were stationed about two miles along the ridge, and one of these companies was overtaken by the Rough Riders. They seemed to me to be almost exhausted, and five or six of them were stretched out at full length by the side of the trail. . . .

"At last the summit was reached. Looking back I could see the little village still in the deep shadow of the hills, the blackened ruins of the houses which the shells from the fleet had destroyed. . . .

"'Guns to the front! Machine guns to the front!' came down the line, and almost immediately after a shrill 'yip yip' was heard from the rear, and four mules packed with the barrels and tripods of the Colts came on a quick trot along the trail, followed by the gun detail. The troopers looked at each other as they passed. 'I recken they've struck some Spaniards,' said one. 'Don't you wish you was back at Bill William's Forks?' . . .

"The trail led into a heavy growth of maingua interspersed with forest trees hung with broad-leaved vines, some of which had been blown down and obstructed [it]. . . . The progress was slow. At times there was hardly room for more than a single file in the trail and there would be a halt to allow for this formation. There were other halts to await the return of the Cuban scouts sent forward to reconnoiter, though these were seldom long. The column seemed to be cautiously feeling its way."

Along the valley road, the column under General Young advanced more rapidly. Lieutenant C. McK. Saltzman, who commanded the advanced guard, recalled: "About 7:30 in the morning the command halted in an open glade to rest. Captain

A. L. Mills, the brigade adjutant . . . went forward about 150
yards to a point near the ruins of an old Spanish house with a
sun dial on the side, which will be remembered by all who participated in this engagement. He sent word back to me in a few
minutes that he had seen a Spanish outpost to our left front."
General Young formed his cavalry squadrons into an irregular
battle line, sent a Cuban scout to inform Colonel Wood, and
waited almost long enough for the Rough Riders to form a
junction with his troops. When General Wheeler arrived,
Young pointed out to him "the Spanish breastworks of loosely
piled up flat stones on the crest of a prominent hill some 800
yards to the front." Major William D. Beach, chief engineer of
the Cavalry Division, described in detail what ensued:

"There was some uncertainty as to whether the straw hats
visible over the breastworks were the head gear of Cubans or
Spaniards. General Wheeler solved the problem by directing
the commander of the Hotchkiss one-pounder gun to open fire
on them which he did, the first shot drawing volleys from the
distant breastworks and more destructive volleys from a nearer
wall on our left front.

"At the opening shot, I jotted down the time (8:15 A.M.) in
my note book, as I had done many times in maneuvers, but my
book appears a blank after the first entry, for the firing on both
sides immediately became very heavy, so much so in fact that
General Wheeler remarked that he remembered no heavier
musketry fire in any action he was in during the Civil War.

"The first casualty—an enlisted man of the 1st Cavalry—
occurred very near to where General Wheeler and I were standing and he went at once to the man, pulled open his shirt to see
where he had been hit; an act on the part of a Major General that
struck me at the time as very strange. But casualties were soon
occurring with startling frequency and all indications seemed to
point to a long continued action with a doubtful outcome. The
Brigade Commander very soon had his entire supports and

reserves deployed, and from the heavy firing on our left, we knew that Colonel Wood's regiment was likewise heavily engaged.

"After what seemed to be an interminable time and when our casualties were rapidly increasing, I said to General Wheeler, 'We have nine big regiments of Infantry only a few miles back on the road. Let me send to General Lawton for one of them and close this action up.' He hesitated but finally said, 'All right!' So I called the mounted orderly . . . [who] started back at a gallop.

"The day wore on, dragged terribly in fact and I for one was consumed with anxiety and apprehension as to the outcome of the fight for our 400 men were *not* advancing and we *were* piling up casualties; eight men killed and three officers and twenty or more men wounded. At that time, at our end of the line, with just one medical officer and one hospital corps man to attend them, this was not pleasing to contemplate. . . . Time crawled, it did not fly; the sun seemed to stand still as in the days of Joshua of old, and it was too awfully hot and oppressive for words. There was little to do in the way of transmitting orders. The entire force was deployed and in action so that the only work my hands found to do was assisting the wounded back to the dressing station; the officers and men of the 1st and 10th Cavalry Squadrons were old hands at their business and needed no encouragement.

"Finally after what seemed an age, the head of the Infantry column sent by Lawton to our assistance hove in sight and simultaneously the Spanish force retreated toward Santiago. As the firing grew fainter, General Wheeler sprang to his feet and shouted, 'We've got the Yankees on the run.' . . .

"With the point of the Infantry column sent by Lawton to our assistance was dear old Wagner. . . . Turning . . . to me Wagner said, 'What time is it?' I thoughtlessly said, 'I don't know . . . but I should judge along in the middle of the afternoon.' I noticed that Wagner look mystified and it occurred to me to look at my watch which I did, and then held it to my ear thinking it had stopped. The watch was ticking industriously and recorded the time as 9:20. It had been just an hour and five minutes since the first shot, but as Colonel Roosevelt afterwards remarked, 'It was a full hour.'"

Meanwhile the untried Rough Riders, none of whom had so much as fired his new Krag rifle, were proving their mettle under even more difficult conditions, against Spanish troops they scarcely ever saw. Colonel Leonard Wood reported the next day:

"At 7:10 our advanced point discovered what they believed to be signs of the immediate presence of the enemy. The command was halted and the troops deployed to the right and left in open skirmish order and the command ordered to advance carefully. The firing began almost immediately, and the extent of firing on each flank indicated that we had encountered a very heavy force. Two additional troops were deployed on the right and left, thus leaving only three troops in reserve. It was soon apparent that [the Spanish] lines were overlapping us on both flanks. Two other troops were rapidly deployed, one on the right and one on the left, which gave our line a length about equal to their own. The firing about this time was exceedingly heavy, much of it at very short range, but on account of the heavy undergrowth comparatively few men were injured at this time. It was about this time that Captain Capron was mortally wounded. The firing on his immediate front was terrific. The remaining troop was sent to the front and the order given to advance very slowly.

"Men and officers behaved splendidly and advanced, slowly forcing back the enemy on the right flank. We captured a small blockhouse and drove the enemy out of a very strong position in the rocks. We were now able to distinguish their line, which had taken a new position about 800 or 1,000 yards in length and about 300 yards in front of us. The firing was exceedingly heavy here again, and it was here that we had a good many men wounded and several officers. Our men continued to advance in very good order and steadily forced the Spanish line back.

"We now began to get heavy fire from a ridge on our right, which enfiladed our line. This ridge was the position which was being attacked by two squadrons of the regular cavalry, and was held in very strong force by the Spanish in small rock forts along its entire length, supported by two machine guns.

"Having cleared our right flank we were able to pay some attention to the Spanish on the . . . ridge, and centered upon it the fire of two troops. This fire, with the attacking force on the other side, soon completed the evacuation of this end of the ridge, and the regular assault completed the evacuation along the entire length of the ridge. Of the Spaniards who retreated from the ridge some few fell into line, but apparently only remained there a moment, when large masses of them were seen to retreat rapidly, and we were able to distinguish parties carrying litters of wounded men.

"At this time my detached troop had moved out to the left to take the right end of the Spanish line in flank. . . . As soon as this troop gained its position 'Cease firing and advance' was ordered. Our men advanced within 300 yards of the enemy, when we again opened heavy fire. The Spanish line broke under this fire and retreated rapidly. . . . This left us in complete possession of the entire Spanish position."

For the soldiers, it was a bewildering encounter. Trooper Cosby wrote his mother: "Today we had the first brush with the enemy. . . . We went blindly down a hill, I heard the scream or whine of bullets, saw dust fly & heard little explosions. I did not see the enemy or smoke but we fired a couple of rounds in their direction to try our guns. We did this for 3 hours tramping up and down as fast as we could. The perspiration simply rolled, the boys got reckless and threw off everything but their cartridge belts. I felt perfectly cool, never more so."

For the commanders, Wood and Roosevelt, it was a splendid opportunity to demonstrate their capacity for bold leadership. "Both . . . disdained to take advantage of shelter or cover from the enemy's fire while any of their men remained exposed to it," General Young reported, "an error of judgment, but happily on the heroic side." One bullet seared Wood's wrist and severed his gold cufflinks; another hit a palm tree so close to Roosevelt's head that it splattered splinters into his ear and eye. Richard Harding Davis ranged at their side almost as a third (and more experienced) commander. He was the first to spot Spanish troops and point them out to Wood; at one point he picked up a rifle and fired a few shots at them. Wood cited Davis in his report, and Davis more than reciprocated in his dispatches. Indeed, he credited the overall victory at Las Guásimas to the Rough Riders' final charge:

"Toward the last, the firing from the enemy sounded less near, and the bullets passed much higher. Roosevelt, who had picked up a carbine and was firing occasionally to give the direction to the others, determined upon a charge. Wood at the other end of the line, decided at the same time upon the same manoeuvre. It was called 'Wood's bluff' afterward, for he had nothing to back it with; while to the enemy it looked as though his whole force was but the skirmish-line in advance of a regiment. The Spaniards naturally could not believe that this thin line which suddenly broke out of the bushes and from behind the trees and came cheering out into the hot sunlight in full view, was the entire fighting force against it. They supposed the regiment was coming close on its heels . . . they fired a few parting volleys and broke and ran. . . . As we knew it was only a bluff, the first cheer was wavering, but the sound of our own voices was so comforting that the second cheer was a howl of triumph."

Soon after the fighting ended, the Ninth Cavalry arrived to reinforce the Rough Riders. "As they had come along the trail," wrote Harris of the Chicago *Record*, "[they] had met the wounded making their way back to Siboney—either hobbling slowly along with the poor assistance of a stick picked up on the wayside or mounted on one of the few mules that had been taken to the front—and the sight of the white, pain-distorted faces and the blood-stained garments had stirred them to a veritable battle fury. But their chance was to come later."

The casualties shocked Burr McIntosh because he felt it had been a needless battle. The joking manner in which some of the soldiers referred to the dead shocked him even more. On his way to Las Guásimas, he met an officer who told him Hamilton Fish was dead. "It was several minutes before I felt like standing to resume the march," McIntosh wrote. The first dead he saw were of the First and Tenth Cavalry; one of the soldiers, spying someone he knew, remarked, "He said they couldn't ketch *him*, and they got him the first one!" Several others laughed. McIntosh went on to the Rough Riders' camp, and finally located the body of Fish next to that of another dead soldier. He lifted the blanket to look at his face: "After taking the photograph of the two bodies, I heard someone laughing. Looking to the right about fifteen feet I saw a group, apparently discussing the events of the day. I took a photograph of it, and then another to show the distance from the two bodies. The photographs were taken with a heart filled with resentful bitterness. It was all 'war,' and time has shown to me that one should be able to drink to 'the next one who dies,' but felt a resentment toward certain of those men, who were joking with that boy's body lying within a few feet of them—a resentment which I never expect to be able to overcome."

McIntosh in his revulsion against war was being quite unfair to the notable group of officers and correspondents whom he photographed. They were indeed, as most of them made clear in their writings, dismayed at the losses. But they recognized, as the main target of McIntosh's resentment, Roosevelt, later wrote, that war was a grim business. Roosevelt paid lavish individual tribute to each of the men lost, especially to Fish and Capron, "two as gallant men as ever wore uniform." He did observe something that McIntosh did not quite fathom:

"I did not see any sign among the fighting men, whether wounded or unwounded, of the very complicated emotions assigned to their kind by some of the realistic modern novelists who have written about battles. At the front everyone behaved quite simply and took things as they came, in a matter-of-course way; but there was doubtless, as is always the case, as good deal of panic and confusion in the rear where the wounded, the stragglers, a few of the packers, and two or three newspaper correspondents were."

From these men in the rear, Roosevelt pointed out, "the first reports sent back to the coast were of a most alarming character, describing, with minute inaccuracy, how we had run into an ambush."

Soon after the false reports, the wounded began to arrive among the excited troops and newspapermen in Siboney. A correspondent not expected to live, Edward Marshall, to the astonishment of bystanders was carried in on a litter singing snatches of "On the Banks of the Wabash." Marshall later wrote:

"I saw many men shot. Every one went down in a lump without cries, without jumping in the air, without throwing up hands. They just went down like clods in the grass.

"There is much that is awe-inspiring about the death of soldiers on the battle-field. . . . The man lives, he is strong, he is vital, every muscle in him is at its fullest tension when, suddenly, 'chug' he is dead. That 'chug' of the bullets striking flesh is nearly always plainly audible . . . I did not hear the bullet shriek that killed Hamilton Fish . . . I did not hear the bullet shriek which hit me.

"This bit of steel came diagonally from the left. I was standing in the open, and, from watching our men in front, had turned partially to see Roosevelt and his men on the right. . . . 'Chug' came the bullet and I fell into the long grass, as much like a lump as had the other fellows whom I had seen go down. There was no pain, no surprise. The tremendous shock so dulled my sensibilities that it did not occur to me that anything extra-ordinary had happened. . . .

"Finally three soldiers found me, and, putting half a shelter-tent under me, carried me to the shade. There were several wounded men there before me. The first-aid men came along, learned that my wound was at the side and had shattered the spine, and shaking their heads gravely, gave me a weak solution of ammonia as a stimulant. . . . [The surgeon] told me I was about to die. The news was not pleasant, but it did not interest me particularly."

Marshall survived, but only after long hospitalization and the loss of a leg. For seven Rough Riders who died there was burial the next morning in a grave at the summit of the trail to Las Guásimas. A brother-in-law of Thomas A. Edison, Theodore Westwood Miller, recorded in his diary: "The men were covered with branch-es and sticks, then the dirt thrown on. Ham Fish was the body at the end of the grave. . . . It was a very impressive occasion. The bugle was blown as a parting salute, instead of firing, and the troops were dismounted." Less than a week later, Miller himself was mortally wounded, and on July 8 buried in a similar grave.

Despite death and the imminence of death, the troops had to occupy themselves with eating, bathing, and resting as best they could.

For the command, there was time to evaluate the battle. The Americans, with fewer than a thousand men, had opposed about fifteen hundred Spaniards behind fortifications (not counting reserves on either side). They lost sixteen men killed and fifty-two wounded, compared with ten Spanish killed and twenty-five wounded.

Shafter must have felt some personal dismay that Wheeler had precipitated an engagement. Shafter would have preferred to depend upon seasoned regulars rather than dismounted cavalry, some of whom were green volunteers, and to have placed in the forefront General H. W. Lawton, who had once nursed him

Left flank of Rough Riders charging blockhouse, by Howard Chandler Christy

R.H. Davis asleep, far left; Wheeler (with star on shoulder) talking to Wood (back to camera); Roosevelt (in suspenders) with Caspar Whitney

through yellow fever. But Wheeler had not disobeyed orders (since they were probably not written until the battle was over) and he had not acted rashly (no one could have expected Linares to be so foolish as to order Las Guásimas abandoned without a fight).

Consequently, Shafter sent the usual congratulations, then assuaged his feelings by warning Wheeler not to bring on another engagement. The battle had heightened the morale of the American troops and brought bursts of enthusiasm in the United States, especially for the newspapermen's heroes, Roosevelt and Wood.

The occupation of Las Guásimas and the area beyond, stretching to the fortifications guarding Santiago, was an essential prelude to any large-scale attack on the city. The narrow road, along which so many of the casualties of the First and Tenth Cavalry had occurred, had to be improved immediately before supplies could be moved forward.

The Quartermaster Department under Colonel Charles F. Humphrey immediately went to work on the road. He has reminisced: "That part between Siboney and Santiago was particularly bad, as it passed over a range of high ground and through depressions, ravines, water courses and small rivers. There were no bridges, and cuts in the hilly portions, and for long distances on nearly level ground, were deep, having apparently been cut down by their long usage, constant erosion, and the effects of heavy rainfalls. . . . The amount of work done was very great, resulting in the material improvement of the old road by corduroying with brush, filling depressions, removing boulders, bridging streams, and cutting through woods, and roughly making new road in part. With all this work done upon it, however, it was at no time in really good order, and a part of the time . . . it was all but impassable, thus rendering it most difficult to meet the demands from the front. . . .

"Much . . . of the road . . . was so narrow, deeply cut, and with such precipitous sides that from first to last wagons could not pass on it, nor could a mounted man pass a wagon, but it was impossible to widen it or build a new road by any other route. Therefore, the moving of pack and wagon trains leaving Siboney and the front had to be timed, and with all care possible temporary blockades occurred, especially when the sick and wounded were being brought to the rear."

Shortages of experienced packers to run the mule trains and upsets of the six-mule wagons increased the transportation snarl. Behind that was the slowness in unloading supplies because of the lack of adequate docks and lighters. As a result, wrote Roosevelt, "we were not given quite the proper amount of food, and what we did get, like most of the clothing issued us, was fitter for the Klondyke than for Cuba. We got enough salt pork and hard-tack for the men, but not the full ration of coffee and sugar, and nothing else."

For several days, the scarcity of supplies halted further advance. Until sufficient of them had been loaded at Siboney so that the expedition would not starve if a hurricane drove the ships away, there was real danger. Until the wagons and packers had taken sufficient munitions and provisions inland, Shafter did not want to begin the big attack upon Santiago.

8

Assault on El Caney

The twin battles of El Caney and San Juan Hill on July 1, 1898, decided whether the American expeditionary force in Cuba would succeed or fail. It was a close decision.

A week earlier, on the afternoon of the victory at Las Guásimas, the American troops moved tantalizingly close to Santiago. From a point a half mile beyond Sevilla, "Fighting Joe" Wheeler reported, "We can see Santiago very plainly from this point, about seven or eight miles distant. The country appears level for six miles this side the city except for heights on the south which extend to within three miles of Santiago, and from which the city can be shelled. These hills now appear deserted. The country is fairly open, a good tract for campaigning over."

The hills were not deserted. It was to these that General Linares had withdrawn his forces, who were working energetically to strengthen their fortifications, and from the hills, the

Spanish could command the open country stretching toward Sevilla. While the Spanish prepared for battle, for six days the American troops waited, not reconnoitering, not cutting new trails through the jungle, not interfering with the Spaniards in any way. They received no orders to do these things; Wheeler was warned not to precipitate a new engagement. Instead, they hungrily foraged for food, waited eagerly for each pack train bringing meager rations, and being out of tobacco, irritatedly tried to beg it from the Cubans. John Black Atkins, a British correspondent, wrote, "When the thousands of insurgents who were landed at Siboney filed up the road to the front the soldiers sat by the wayside and demanded tobacco. 'Tobacco,' 'Tobacco,' they said all along the line. The Cubans might have taken the word as a welcome; smiling, they waved back their salutations, and continued to smoke their cheroots."

The troops, still tired from the long confinement on the transports, were too occupied with keeping fed and dry to complain. Richard Harding Davis regarded the inaction as little short of criminal:

"On the 27th of June, a long, yellow pit opened in the hillside of San Juan, and in it we could see straw sombreros rising and bobbing up and down, and under the shade of the blockhouse, blue-coated Spaniards strolling leisurely about or riding forth on little white ponies to scamper over the hills. . . . Rifle-pits were growing in length and in number, and in plain sight from the hill of El Poso, the enemy was intrenching himself at San Juan and at the little village of El Caney to the right, where he was marching through the streets. But no artillery was sent to El Poso hill to drop a shell among the busy men at work among the trenches, or to interrupt the street parades in El Caney."

This was the only advantage the Spaniards still possessed. Even before the landing of the American troops, the defenders of Santiago were hard pressed. Supplies were short, and during the spring, the merchants, fearing army confiscation, had prudently sold off their stocks of provisions without replenishing them. In May, before the blockade, a German ship had unloaded fourteen thousand sacks of rice; aside from this, there was scarcely food to last the troops and inhabitants of Santiago for a month. As the city came under siege, hunger was a threat for those within, as fever was for the attackers without.

Perhaps because of the scarcity of food, General Linares decided not to call in more of the troops scattered throughout the province. On June 22, the day of the Daiquiri landing, thirty-six hundred men began the march from Manzanillo, forty-five miles away. Until they arrived, he had to depend upon a defense force of thirteen thousand men. These, and the number of officers and men, were:

Cuba (Santiago) regiment	1644	Engineers and snappers	411
Asia regiment	1096	Siege artillery	137
San Fernando regiment	822	Mountain artillery	50
Porto Rico regiment	822	Civil guards	137
Talavera regiment	822	Signal corp	72
Constitución regiment	822	Volunteers and firemen	1869
Mobilized troops	2192	Guerrillas	1000
King's regiment (cavalry)	200	Sailors	1000

Along the crest of the hills ringing Santiago, the Spanish engineers, aided by the infantry, had dug more than four thousand yards of trenches and ditches, at most points two or three lines deep, with breastworks and barbed wire to protect them. Most of the dirt had been hauled away, so that there was no clear indication where these lines were. The excavation that Davis watched the Spaniards undertake was only the last strengthening of fortifications upon which they had been working since the end of April. The line of fortifications ran from the bay inland around the city. Capping it were blockhouses, and at the village of El Caney, a stone fort.

From their breastworks on Kettle Hill, the Spaniards aimed their guns and rifles at the edge of the jungle where the two trails opened into the clearing, and waited for the Americans. "Of course, the enemy knows where those two trails leave the wood," General A. R. Chaffee told Davis. "If our men leave the cover and reach the plain from those trails alone they will be piled up so high that they will block the road." Chaffee recommended cutting numerous trails through the jungle and into the clearing, but it was not done. He himself supervised the reconnaissance toward El Caney, and opened two and a half miles of road toward it so that artillery could advance.

By June 30, General Shafter had built up a sufficient store of ammunition and supplies to begin an attack. He was anxious to strike the Spaniards before the reinforcements could arrive from Manzanillo; the insurgents were harassing but not blocking them. In the morning while Generals Lawton and Chaffee explored the area around El Caney, he and his staff, although he was suffering from heat exhaustion, surveyed the Spanish lines from the hill of El Pozo. He could clearly see the fortifications on San Juan Hill, and four miles distant, El Caney.

Shortly after noon, Shafter held a council of war with his division commanders, except for Wheeler, who was ill with a fever. "The plan of battle for July 1st," wrote Shafter's aide-de-camp, Miley, "was to begin the attack at El Caney with one division of infantry and one battery of artillery at daybreak, or as early thereafter as possible, and as soon as the troops at El Caney were well engaged to move against the heights of San Juan with the rest of the command. . . .

"General Lawton's division, with Capron's light battery, was ordered to move on the afternoon of the 30th, taking the road to El Caney, which left the main road to Santiago about one hundred yards in advance of head-quarters camp. That night he was expected to bivouac as near El Caney as practicable and begin the assault upon the place at daylight.

"General Kent and General Sumner were to move their divisions, preceded by Grimes's light battery, along the main road to Santiago, going as far as El Pozo, where all would bivouac for the night. Three days' rations were ordered carried by every one. Gun pits were to be prepared on the heights at El Pozo, and during the night, or early the next morning, Grimes's battery was ordered to be in position there.

"General Bates, at Siboney, was directed to proceed at once to the front and report his brigade, the Third and Twentieth United States Infantry, to the commanding general."

While one of the correspondents, Stephen Bonsal, was gazing from a hillside at Santiago on the afternoon of June 30, he wrote, "I thought I heard the crashing sound of artillery moving along the road. . . . I galloped down the hill, tearing through the bushes and the briers, following through the dusk of the evening the glint of the dying sunlight upon the bright steel jackets of the guns.

"'Cannoneers forward!' I heard the familiar command, and the great crashing noise with which the iron-bound wheels jolted over the rough roads and through the granite bed of the stream. There was no mistake now. Behind the artillery, as far back as the eye could see, the road was thronged with soldiers in heavy marching order. The army was moving at last."

The order did not come until three o'clock to break camp and move forward at four—and all regiments apparently were ordered to march at the same time. Davis reported, "It was as though fifteen regiments were encamped along the sidewalks of Fifth Avenue and were all ordered at the same moment to move into it and march down town. If Fifth Avenue were ten feet wide, one can imagine the confusion."

A half hour earlier the rain had been pouring down. The ground was soaked, and the trees half obscured by mist, but the men were glad to be moving. Ahead of them floated the Signal Corps observation balloon, as it, too, gradually went forward. Wrote Davis:

"Twelve thousand men, with their eyes fixed on a balloon, and treading on each other's heels in three inches of mud, move slowly, and after three hours, it seemed as though every man in the United States was under arms and stumbling and slipping down that trail. The lines passed until the moon rose. They seemed endless, interminable; there were cavalry mounted and dismounted, artillery with cracking whips and cursing drivers, Rough Riders in brown, and regulars, both black and white, in blue. Midnight came, and they were still slipping forward. . . .

"Below us lay the basin a mile and a half in length, and a mile and a half wide, from which a white mist was rising. Near us, drowned under the mist, seven thousand men were sleeping, and, further to the right, General Chaffee's five thousand were laying under the bushes along the trails to El Caney, waiting to march on it and eat it up before breakfast. . . .

"Three miles away, across the basin of mist, we could see the street-lamps of Santiago shining over the San Juan hills. Above us, the tropical moon hung white and clear in the dark purple sky, pierced with millions of white stars. . . . Before the moon rose again, every sixth man who had slept in the mist that night was either killed or wounded."

The first target on the morning of July 1 was to be the small village of El Caney, a hamlet of palm-thatched and tile-roofed buildings on a moderate hill. A stone church, where Cortez was supposed to have prayed the night before he sailed to conquer Mexico, dominated the village; there were loopholes in its walls, and Spanish sharpshooters were stationed in its tower. Five hundred yards southeast of El Caney on a hillock was a stone fort, El Viso, surrounded by trenches and barbed wire and supporting blockhouses. Against the defending Spaniards, who numbered only 520, Shafter sent 6,653 men, nearly half his force, confident that they could reduce the fort in a few minutes, then join the right flank in the main attack upon the fortifications of Santiago. He held his main force in abeyance until

General Lawton could achieve this difficult and unnecessary objective. El Caney was an outpost; the troops had to cross from Santiago in attacking it.

General Shafter assigned only two batteries—four light guns—to reduce the blockhouses and stone fortifications. He assigned two others to bombard San Juan Hill, and kept two others—half of his sixteen guns—in reserve. The guns, one of the artillery officers, Dwight E. Aultman, later wrote, were 3.2-inch field guns, "the latest, and last development of the old non-recoil material, firing unfixed ammunition with black powder charges and unprovided with any of the laying apparatus for indirect fire." At the same time, the French seventy-five-millimeter gun had been developed "with its fixed ammunition, rapid fire and indirect laying. Yet such was our backwardness in military science that the whole Army was ignorant of the tremendous advance in Field Artillery that in 1898 was an accomplished fact."

The artillerymen did their best with the bad equipment. When the novelist of the southern hills, John Fox, Jr., approached El Caney about 6:30 on the morning of July 1, he found the battery commanded by Captain Allyn Capron—whose son of the same name had been killed at Las Guásimas—ready to begin firing:

"The hill had been cleared of bushes, the four guns unlimbered and thrown into position against Caney, the caissons drawn to the rear, the horses gathered into the bushes to one side, and officers, aides, and correspondents walked the length of the hill, or stood in groups watching with field-glasses the red town, the stone fort to the right, and the block-house to the right of it. . . .

"So when a Spanish column of cavalry was sighted in a lane near Caney . . . [they turned out to be Cuban refugees] Captain Capron said, 'Give 'em a shell, boys.' . . . The man with the lanyard gave a quick jerk. There was a cap explosion at the butt of the gun, a bulging white cloud from the muzzle, the trail bounced from its shallow trench, and the wheels whirled back twice on the rebound, and the shell was hissing through the air. . . . Six seconds later a puff of smoke answered beyond the Spanish column where the shell burst. . . .

"No harm seemed near . . . for the shells went wide; but the first shot started the ripping of cloth, the far-away rumble of wagons over cobblestones, or softened stage-hail and stage-thunder all around the block-house, stone fort, and town. At first it was a desultory fire, like the popping of a bunch of fire-crackers . . . and we could hear the hiss of the bullets even that far away. . . . But the powder was smokeless, and we could see nothing other than the straw hats of the little devils in blue, who blazed away from their trenches around the fort, and minded the shells bursting over and around them as little as though they had been bursting snowballs. For the 3.2 inch guns had turned from the Spanish column, after it had ridden quiet-ly out of sight, to the fort, and, with the exception of one gun, the shooting was at first very wild. One shot tore a hole through the wall, then another; another brought down the flag; others tore up the earth at the base of the fort . . . but the rifle-pits were as active as ever, and after throwing a few shells into the town the battery ceased firing." It was about ten o'clock. General Chaffee afterward explained, "There was not sufficient artillery there to demoralize the garrison."

Far from retreating at the first shots, the Spaniards concen-trated a deadly fire on the Americans and Cubans. "General Chaffee's brigade led off the fighting," wrote Herbert Billman for the Chicago *Record*. "With about 200 [actually 50] Cubans under the command of General De Coro he began a lively skir-mish fire upon the enemy's outposts as soon as the dawning light defined his position. For the first hour the firing was scat-tered and occasional. But it soon became evident the Spanish were prepared to make a stubborn resistance. Even the most remote pickets fought our advance with grimmest determination. Only by paces was it possible to push them back from the lines of thicket behind which they shot with the deliberate aim of sharpshooters. When driven from this shelter they took up an annoying position in a blockhouse . . . a thousand yards north of the town, where it was almost impossible to reach them effectively with rifle fire.

"General Chaffee and the Cubans on the right pushed forward steadily, the latter skirmishing on the extreme flank, and moving to a position as far as possible to the westward, so as to cut off the Spanish line of retreat to the hills. General Ludlow's Brigade supported the battery in the front, and advanced rapidly in the face of stubborn opposition, going first to the main Santiago highway and then to a position east of El Caney, where he occupied a sunken trail within fifty yards of the town. The banks of the trail gave him an effective breastwork in the event of his being placed upon the defensive, but it was not deep enough to protect him from the fire of the enemy's sharpshooters hidden within the shambling houses of the town.

"General Ludlow's horse was shot under him, and Colonel Patterson of the Twenty-second received a bad wound. The Second Massachusetts suffered severely, apparently because the Springfield rifle with which the state troops are equipped uses black powder that invariably betrays its position and exposes the soldier to well-directed shots from the enemy. . . .

"By 9 o'clock the battle was in full heat throughout the right. All three bridges had advanced rapidly, Ludlow having pushed within 100 yards of El Caney and drawn fire from a score of outlying houses. This led to sharp volley firing from the regiments occupying the sunken road and to a rain of shrapnel from Capron's battery. Chaffee pushed the Twelfth Infantry beyond the little blockhouse in his path, and was giving and taking volleys from the enemy's several lines of defense as he slowly retreated upon the fort. From this time until 10 o'clock firing on both sides was ceaseless. The Spanish having no cannon in the fort and the [United States] battery upon the hill being beyond the range of the enemy's small arms, our main position was secure. But in the valley there was a continuous rattle of bullets through the foliage of the trees. . . .

"Having by 10 o'clock made his position safe, in the face of opposition infinitely greater than any one looked forward to, General Lawton sent word forward to desist from the attack in order to allow his tired forces to gain much-needed rest after the forced marches of the night before. . . .

"It was not until 1 o'clock that the battle was resumed in earnest. General Ludlow's Brigade in the sunken road started it with blasting volleys directed at the enemy's sharpshooters and a small blockhouse at the edge of the town. General Chaffee followed immediately with renewed activity in his assault on the fort. Though Capron's shells had pierced it through and through, and torn down its flagstaff and colors, still the garrison fought with furious desperation. From trenches below the fort which cannon shot seemed to have no effect upon, they poured repeated volleys at every column showing in their front. . . .

"During Chaffee's last advance upon the fort his brigade suffered most severely. Stretches of cleared land along the hillsides in his front exposed his men to a raking fire from the fort and from a supporting blockhouse a little to the northwest. By quick rushes the Twelfth and Seventeenth got across these dangerous passes, and at 2:30 the former regiment reached the foot of the hill just below the range of fire from the enemy's pits. At the same time Colonel Miles's Brigade reached the western side of the town and was prepared to join in a united assault upon the fort."

At about this time, General Shafter, fearing that the long delay at El Caney might imperil the main thrust at San Juan, sent an order to General Lawton: "I would not bother with little block-houses. They can't harm us. Bates's Brigade and your Division and García should move on the city and form the right of line, going on Sevilla road. Line is now hotly engaged." By the time the order reached General Lawton his troops were so deeply engaged in the final assault that he could not safely withdraw them.

To the soldiers engaged in the hours of combat it was a confusing and frightening conflict. James A. Moss, lieutenant in the Twenty-fifth Infantry, a Negro regiment, vividly described the battle as he saw it. All morning, the Twenty-fifth was held in reserve: shortly after noon, they advanced to the firing line, about eight hundred yards from El Viso:

"The dead, dying and wounded are being taken past to the rear; the wounded and their attendants are telling the Twenty-fifth: 'Give them hell, boys; they've been doing us dirt all morning.'

"A member of the Second Massachusetts, carrying several canteens, and going to the rear for water, says to our soldiers: 'The buggers are hidden behind rocks, in weeds and in underbrush, and we just simply can't locate them; they are shooting our men all to pieces.'

"The procession is, indeed, terrible! Men with arms in slings; men with bandaged legs and bloody faces; men stripped to the waist, with a crimson bandage around the chest or shoulder; men staggering along unaided; men in litters, some groaning, some silent, with hats or blood-stained handkerchiefs over their faces; some dead, some dying! . . .

"The Twenty-fifth's left connects with the Fourth's right.

"'Forward, guide left, march!' is given, and advancing two hundred yards through a grass field, hidden from the enemy's view by a double row of trees, they reach a barbed wire fence. Some of the soldiers are supplied with wire cutters—the command at once cuts its way through, and crossing a lane, enters an open pineapple patch. Ye gods! It is raining lead! The line recoils like a mighty serpent, and then, in confusion, advances again! The Spaniards now see them and are pouring a most mur-

derous fire into their ranks! Men are dropping everywhere! . . .
The bullets are cutting the pineapples under our very feet—the
slaughter is awful! . . .

"The Spaniards are using smokeless powder, and being
under cover, we cannot locate them, A few yards to our left are
high weeds, a few paces to the right, thick underbrush and
trees, a short distance to the front, a veritable jungle—all, for
more than we know, alive with Spaniards. The bullets . . . are
raining into our very faces. A soldier comes running up, and
cries out, 'Lieutenant, we're shooting into our own men!' Mid
the cracking of rifles, the whizzing of bullets, the killing and
wounding of men, and the orders of the officers, great is the
confusion! How helpless, oh, how helpless we feel! Our men are
being shot down under our very feet, and we, their officers, can
do nothing for them. . . .

"The officers in the pineapple patch are now holding a consultation, and decide there is but one thing for United States
Regulars to do—Advance! Advance until they find the enemy!

"The onward movement is just about to start. Lieutenant
McCorkle is under a small cherry tree, kneeling on one knee;
unbuttoning his shirt, he lowers his head and beholds in the pit
of his right arm a ghastly wound, and then, poor fellow, he falls
over, mortally wounded. . . .

"Lieutenants Caldwell and Kinnison have been gradually
working their way up another stream, and are now about two
hundred yards from the fort, and for the first time since the firing line was formed do our men see the Spaniards. . . .

"Lieutenant Hunt's company is firing over the crest of a
hillock fifty yards to the front and right.

"Our firing line is now no more than one hundred and fifty
yards from the fort, and our men are doing grand work. A general fusillading for a few minutes, and then orders are given for
no one but marksmen and sharpshooters to fire. Thirty or forty
of these dead-shots are pouring lead into every rifle-pit, door,

window, and porthole in sight. The earth, brick and mortar are fairly flying! The Spaniards are shaken and demoralized; bareheaded and without rifles, they are frantically running from their rifle-pits to the fort, and from the fort to the rifle-pits! Our men are shooting them down like dogs! A young officer is running up and down, back of the firing line, and waving his hat above his head is exclaiming to the men in the rear: 'Come on, come on, men—we've got 'em on the run!' 'Remember the Maine!' shouts a sergeant. 'Give them hell, men!' cries out an officer. 'There's another,' shouts a soldier—bang! bang! and another Spaniard drops! Four are shot down in the door of the fort!

"A Spaniard appears in the door of the fort, and presents . . . a white flag, but is shot down before the firing line can be controlled. Another takes up the flag, and he, too, falls!"

"The fort has been silenced!

"However, a galling flank fire is now coming from the village and a small block-house on our left. As long as we remain in our present position, we can accomplish but little, as the walls of the block-house are impervious to our bullets. It is, therefore, decided to rush forward and change direction to the left, thus gaining a position facing, and slightly above the block-house.

"The line is now being formed for the final rush—all is ready—they're off.

"One company of the Twelfth Infantry, which has been working its way up on the right, is also rushing up. [It was the Twelfth which led the charge on El Viso.]

"Lieutenant Kinnison is wounded and taken off the field.

"Men are still dropping by the wayside, but on, on, up, up, they go, those dusky boys in blue!

"The line is now occupying its new position—some of our men are shooting into the town, and others are shooting down through the roof of the block-house—the Spaniards are falling over one another to get out!

"The heavy firing has ceased, and after twenty-five or thirty minutes of desultory firing, El Caney itself surrenders!

"Where but a moment ago floated the Spanish flag, now flutters the Stars and Stripes!"

The Spaniards, who had let up their fire because they were running short of ammunition, put up resistance as long as they could. Even after El Viso and the town had been captured, wrote James F. J. Archibald, "the enemy's last stand was at the little thatched fort, surrounded by trenches, at the western entrance of the town on the Santiago road, where a small band of Spaniards held the road for hours and died like heroes. Their officers appeared to court death, for they exposed themselves uselessly while urging their men to fight. General Vara del Rey rode his horse up and down the lines."

In the last minutes of fighting as he was rallying his men in the square before the church, the Spanish commander was hit in the legs by a bullet; as he was being helped onto a stretcher he was struck again in the head, and died instantly. The Spaniards lost 235 killed and wounded; 120 were taken prisoner. In contrast, the Americans lost 441 men—81 killed and 360 wounded.

Both sides expressed admiration for the gallantry of the other. The Americans buried General Vara del Rey with military honors. One of his staff officers, in return, declared:

"I have never seen anything to equal the courage and dash of those Americans, who, stripped to the waist, offering their naked breasts to our murderous fire, literally threw themselves on our trenches—on the very muzzles of our guns. We had the advantage of position, and mowed them down by the hundreds; but they never retreated or fell back an inch. As one man fell, shot through the heart, another would take his place, with grim determination and unflinching devotion to duty in every line of his face. Their gallantry was heroic."

The Spanish troops had suffered frightfully as they fought to hold off more than ten times their number of American

"Blockhouse No. 14, which gave us so much trouble"

General Joaquin Vara del Rey, defender of El Caney

"An Awful Tragedy of the Spanish War," by Christy

attackers. At two o'clock, Capron had moved his battery to within one thousand yards of El Viso, and did serious damage to it. Charles M. Sheldon, a British correspondent for *Leslie's Weekly*, drew a pencil sketch of the interior, and wrote:

"It was simply punched to pieces. . . . The wall were between two and three feet thick, and inside the fort were whitewashed sheds for the protection of the soldiers against the weather. The garrision was practically all killed, and lay about among the debris of splintered and tumbled walls. Nearly all of them were wounded, not once, but many times. Looking down on the position from which we attacked, the wonder simply is that we were not absolutely annihilated. There is no doubt that if the Spaniards had held their stone fort at Caney with sharpshooters we would have been defeated with terrible loss, because our artillery was entirely inadequate for the work before us."

The British military attaché, Captain Lee, inquired, according to one officer, "whether it was customary with us to assault blockhouses and rifle pits before they had been searched by artillery; to which reply was made, 'Not always.'" Lee later lamented the heavy bloodshed. "This was a heavy price to pay for the possession of an outlying post, defended by an inferior force," he wrote, "but it only bore out the well-known military axiom that the attack on a fortified village cannot succeed, without great loss of life, unless the assailants are strong in artillery. . . . That the attack succeeded was entirely due to the magnificent courage and endurance of the infantry officers and men."

The gory realities of the slaughter in El Caney left little room for the romance of which the war correspondents had dreamed and for which their readers back home hungered. James F. J. Archibald, making his way through the squalid streets among the terrified people, wrote a stirring dispatch which, for the most part, must have stayed close to the unpleasant facts, but one incident, later illustrated by Christy, seemed modeled on one of the popular novels of the time:

"In one old house, that looked as though it might belong to a wealthy family, was a most tragic scene. On the floor was the body of a beautiful young girl, dressed richly in a loose gown of light material, and sticking into an ugly wound in her breast was a knife, while the blood had formed a black pool on the tiled floor. A few feet away a Spanish officer sat with his head on the table, drunk. Through the barred window one could see the little old church, and at the opposite side the open door led into a beautiful court-yard. No amount of shaking could arouse the man, and he slept on, heedless of the evidence of a horrible crime. I had him carried away, and never saw him again. I pulled the knife from the body and drew a sheet over it, and wondered if there was no limit to the horror of war."

9

Up San Juan Hill

The charge up San Juan Hill and its flanking outpost, Kettle Hill, seemed in 1898 to be one of the most heroic deeds in American military history. It crowned with luster the military reputation of one of its chief participants, Theodore Roosevelt, who in little more than three years became president of the United States. As years went by, the blundering inefficiency of the high command overshadowed the courageous hardihood of the troops; the energetic resistance of the Spaniards was forgotten. In the retelling, the battle seemed something of a skylark, almost comic in nature, obscuring the grim and desperate struggle that bloody day.

While General Lawton was flinging his troops at the stone fort and blockhouses of El Caney, the remaining eighty-four hundred American troops had to fight almost without overall direction against the main body of the Spanish forces. General

Linares so badly assigned his men that only about twelve hundred of them met the attack, but they were well entrenched, and the Americans seriously deficient in artillery.

General Shafter was too ill and, perhaps, as his critics charged, too far beyond his depth to give effective direction to the battle. "Not since the campaign of Crassus against the Parthians has there been so criminally incompetent a General as Shafter," Roosevelt protested to Senator Lodge on July 5; "and not since the expedition against Walcheren has there been grosser mismanagement than in this. The battle simply fought itself."

"At three o'clock on the morning of July 1," reminisced Lieutenant Colonel E. J. McClernand, Shafter's adjutant general, "I entered the tent of the Commanding General. He said he was very ill as a result of his exertions in the terrifically hot sun of the previous day, and feared he would not be able to participate as actively in the coming battle as he had intended. He then asked if the staff officers understood the plan of battle, and upon being assured they did he directed me to establish Battle Headquarters at the El Pozo House and Hill, and said he would send staff officers to carry orders. . . .

"Sometime after the artillery had opened at El Caney and the roar of small arms indicated the Infantry there was hotly engaged, General Sumner, in command of the dismounted Cavalry Division, which had been formed in column in rear of El Pozo Hill, and in the underbrush near the road leading to the San Juan River, came to Battle Headquarters and asked when the order to advance would be given. His attention was called to the understanding with Lawton. [Lawton had said at the council of war, "McClernand, do not order the other divisions to attack until I get up. Give me time to reduce El Caney."] . . . So far there had been no firing from El Pozo or from the enemy in its front.

"However, as time went on and the roar of battle continued at El Caney, it became evident that Lawton might be materially

Colonel Theodore Roosevelt

Colonel John Jacob Astor watching effect of shell

Balloon with Lts. Williams and Campbell in basket

delayed; and fearing that the enemy at Santiago, if left longer disengaged, might detach to beat him before the troops near El Pozo could cross the river and form for attack, the Cavalry Division was ordered forward with instructions to cross the San Juan and to deploy to the right, with its left resting on the Santiago road. . . .

"General Kent came up in person, to El Pozo, and I pointed out to him the position he was to attack on San Juan Heights, and added that after fording the river his division would deploy to the left with its right resting on the Santiago road. The division was following close on the heels of the Cavalry."

The evening before, the Rough Riders had been marched to the abandoned farmhouse and sugar factory on El Pozo Hill. Since Wood had been promoted to brigade commander, Roosevelt was in charge of the Rough Riders. Roosevelt wrote:

"As the sun rose the men fell in, and at the same time a battery of field-guns was brought up on the hill-crest just beyond, between us and toward Santiago. It was a fine sight to see the great horses straining under the lash as they whirled the guns up the hill and into position. . . .

"Our guns opened, and at the report great clouds of white smoke hung on the ridge crest. For a minute or two there was no response. . . . There was a peculiar whistling, singing sound in the air, and immediately afterward the noise of something exploding over our heads. It was shrapnel from the Spanish batteries. We sprung to our feet and leaped on our horses. Immediately afterward a second shot came which burst directly above us; and then a third. From the second shell one of the shrapnel bullets dropped on my wrist, hardly breaking the skin, but raising a bump about as big as a hickory-nut. The same shell wounded four of my regiment . . . and two or three of the regulars were also hit. . . . Another shell exploded right in the middle of the Cubans, killing and wounding a good many, while the remainder scattered like guinea-hens. . . . I at once hustled my regiment over the crest of the hill into the thick underbrush, where I had no little difficulty in getting them together again into column."

"It was thoroughly evident that the Spaniards had the range of everything in the country," reported Frederic Remington. He had been sketching Grimes's horses coming up the hill, but fled with the rest. "Some gallant soldiers and some as daring correspondents as it is my pleasure to know did their legs proud there. The tall form of Major John Jacob Astor moved in my front in jack-rabbit bounds. Prussian, English, and Japanese correspondents, artists, all the news, and much high-class art and literature, were flushed, and went straddling up the hill. . . . All this time no one's glass could locate the fire of the Spanish guns and we could see Capron's smoke miles away on our right. Smoky powder belongs with arbalists and stone axes . . . in museums."

At 8:20, Grimes had begun firing at the fortifications on San Juan Hill. From a distance of twenty-five hundred yards he was not able to do any damage, and suffered from the return fire which the smoke from the black powder attracted. After three quarters of an hour he ceased firing, resuming later to protect the advance of Sumner's division, moving toward San Juan Hill.

General Shafter was too ill in the morning to move to El Pozo Hill, but from a hill a mile further back, watched the activity far in the distance both at El Caney and the San Juan Heights. By telephone he kept in touch with his adjutant general, McClernand, on El Pozo, who gave instructions to the army. For fear the Spanish might reinforce the garrison at El Caney or even defeat the Americans there, he ordered Sumner's and Kent's divisions to rush along the jungle trail to San Juan Hill as rapidly as possible.

There began a tragic procession along the road which the Spaniards already knew the Americans must use. With incredible foolhardiness, the troops marked their precise whereabouts with the observation balloon, which they again sent up. The balloon, with Lieutenant Colonel Derby, the chief engineer officer, and Major Maxfield of the signal corps in the basket, was pulled along first by wagon, then by men hauling the guy ropes. General Shafter's aide-de-camp, Miley, wrote: "Winding their way among the troops the balloon was soon within a few hundred yards of the Aguadores River. The enemy's musketry fire was already becoming quite spirited, but when the balloon reached this point it was opened upon by a heavy fire from field-guns, and the musketry fire also increased. The third shell or shrapnel fired at the balloon struck it, and the next one tore it so badly that it at once descended. Time enough, however, was afforded Colonel Derby to discover a road leading from the main road to the left and crossing the Aguadores River four or five hundred yards farther down the stream. This was a most opportune discovery, as the main road was congested with troops and the fire so heavy as to tend to demoralize the men. . . . General Kent . . . at once turned his division into [the side road]."

"The front had burst out with a roar like a brushfire," wrote Stephen Crane. "The balloon was dying, dying a gigantic and public death before the eyes of two armies. It quivered, sank, faded into the trees amid the flurry of a battle that was suddenly and tremendously like a storm.

"The American battery thundered behind the men with a shock that seemed likely to tear the backs of their heads off. The Spanish shrapnel fled on a line to their left, swirling and swishing in supernatural velocity. The noise of the rifle bullets broke in their faces like the noise of so many lamp-chimneys or sped overhead in swift cruel spitting. And at the front the battle-sound, as if it were simply music, was beginning to swell and swell until the volleys rolled like a surf."

Along a mile of jungle road, men not seeing the enemy, not even seeing the fortifications on the hills defending Santiago, came under fire. First Lieutenant John J. Pershing, of the Negro Tenth Cavalry, had helped hurry his men along it before the firing became heavy:

"The road . . . follows, tortuous and narrow, along the river through the swampy jungle, then crosses the river and passes toward and between the San Juan Hills. . . . The regiment moved slowly along this road under the scorching sun and sweltered; a few men were overcome with heat; already, an occasional bullet nipped a leaf above our heads. Impatient at delay the regiment and brigade finally swung past the waiting infantry and moved farther down the road. . . .

"When the Tenth Cavalry arrived at the crossing of the San Juan River, the balloon had become lodged in the treetops above and the enemy had just begun to make a target of it—no doubt correctly supposing that our troops were moving along this road and were near at hand. A converging fire from all the works within range opened upon us that was terrible in its effect; the Seventy-first New York, which lay in a sunken road near the ford, became demoralized and well-nigh stampeded; our mounted officers dismounted, them men stripped off at the roadside everything possible, and prepared for business.

"We were posted for a time in the bed of the stream to the right, directly under the balloon, and stood in water to our waists awaiting orders to deploy. Remaining there under this galling fire of exploding shrapnel and deadly mauser volleys the minutes seemed like hours. . . . General Wheeler and a part of his staff stood mounted a few moments in the middle of the stream. Just as I raised my hat to salute . . . a piece of bursting shell struck between us and covered us both with water.

"Pursuant to orders from its commander with myself as guide, the second squadron of the Tenth forced its way through wire fence and almost impenetrable thicket to its position. . . . The regiment was soon deployed as skirmishers in an opening across the river to the right of the road, and our line . . . being

partly visible from the enemy's position, their fire was turned
upon us and we had to lie down in the grass a few minutes for
safety. Two officers of the regiment were wounded here, and
there were frequent calls for the surgeon; casualties still
occurred and there was a delay in the order to move forward.
Whatever may have been the intention as to the part to be
played by the cavalry division on that day, the officers present
were not long in deciding the part their commands should play."

At the river crossing, General Kent and General Hawkins
held an impromptu consultation with Shafter's aide-de-camp,
Miley: "General Kent said that he and General Hawkins considered that the key to the position was a height directly in
front of us, crowned by a block-house . . . Fort San Juan Hill.
The two Generals advanced far enough to gain an uninter-
rupted view of this place, and both decided that the principal
attack should be directed against it, and General Hawkins with
his brigade was assigned to the attack."

The deploying of troops was slow under heavy fire which
reached a half mile back along the jungle road. General Sumner
took Wheeler's cavalry units, temporarily under his command,
across the bloody ford in the Aguadores (called the San Juan
River by the troops), and gradually put them in position to the
right, directly in front of the most advanced Spanish position,
Kettle Hill. As the Rough Riders pushed by the New York
Seventy-first, the men cheered Colonel Roosevelt. He retorted
rather tartly, "Don't cheer, but fight, now's the time to fight."

Colonel Charles A. Wikoff pushed his men single-file along
the trail past the recumbent Seventy-first, which, made up of
green troops armed with black-powder rifles, had been put in
the lead and was refusing to go forward. Their casualties were
as heavy as if they had fought. Wikoff took his men across the
San Juan River to an open meadow stretching to the San Juan
fortifications no more than five hundred yards away. Ignoring
the heavy fire, Colonel Wikoff was directing the Thirteenth

Infantry to their positions when he was hit, and died in a few minutes. His first two successors in command of the brigade were each wounded almost immediately. The position of the Sixth Infantry under General Hawkins was even more desperate; in ten minutes a quarter of its men were casualties, and it had to withdraw to a protected site. The Spaniards were inflicting frightful punishment upon the American troops before they could even get into firing position. Malcolm McDowell of the Chicago *Record* reported, "Our men continually cried, 'Show us those — — —! For God's sake don't keep us here to be shot without giving us a show.' And they cursed and raved because they could see nothing to shoot at—nothing but the cleared hilltop, and what looked like a long mile of freshly thrown-up earth."

Quantities of wounded were brought to the dressing station that George J. Newgarden, regimental surgeon of the Third Cavalry, had established on the riverbank at the "bloody ford." Unfortunately, the protection from the shot and shell was slight. "It is a marvel that every living thing thereabouts was not either killed or wounded," Newgarden reminisced. "The wounded came pouring in from over the bank in a steady stream, some limping, some hopping, others holding their arms to their sides or abdomen, many using the rifle as a crutch or support, and a number carried in by their comrades. . . . The capacity of the dressing-station was very soon strained to its utmost."

"One beautiful boy was brought in by two tough, stringy, hairy old soldiers, his head hanging down behind," Remington reported. "His shirt was off, and a big red spot shone brilliantly against his marblelike skin. They laid him tenderly down, and the surgeon stooped over him. His breath came in gasps. The doctor laid his arms across his breast, and shaking his head, turned to a man who held a wounded foot up to him, dumbly imploring aid, as a dog might. It made my nerves jump, looking at that grewsome hospital, sand-covered, with bleeding men."

Stephen Crane, passing by, came upon a fellow student of years before: "I looked down into a miserable huddle at Bloody Bend, a huddle of hurt men, dying men, dead men. And there I saw Reuben McNab, a corporal in the 71st New York Volunteers, and with a hole through his lung. Also, several holes through his clothing. 'Well, they got me,' he said in greeting. Usually they said that. . . . I had looked upon five hundred men with stolidity, or with a conscious indifference which filled me with amazement. But the apparition of Reuben McNab, the schoolmate, lying there in the mud, with a hole through his lung, awed me into stutterings, set me trembling with a sense of terrible intimacy with this war which theretofore I could have believed was a dream—almost."

"The charges for the dynamite gun had been left at the dressing-station," wrote George C. Musgrave. "Several shells burst near by, and an explosion of the dangerous ammunition was imminent, when Basil Ricketts, of the Rough Riders, and two troopers hurriedly dug a trench for the boxes. Bullets were falling around in all directions, and the enemy's sharpshooters also opened upon the little party. We had lifted the cases into the pit, when Ricketts fell, shot in the groin." He would not allow himself to be carried to the dressing station until Glackens and two others had covered the munition cases.

For even the bravest men, the long wait under fire was an ordeal. Frank Knox, who had left his study for the ministry to join the Rough Riders, wrote his parents, "Now it is hard enough to face those ugly bullets with your own carbine smoking in your hand, but it becomes doubly hard when you lay under a hell of fire and can't fire a shot to reply. Such was our situation all the morning—just keeping a few yards in the rear of the firing line, but not allowed to join it. We had not been on the field five minutes before our men began to get hit on the left and on the right of me. Fifteen minutes after the fight opened Captain O'Neill of Troop H was killed, one of the finest captains in our regiment."

O'Neill "had a theory that an officer ought never to take cover—" wrote Roosevelt, "a theory which was, of course, wrong, though in a volunteer organization the officers should certainly expose themselves very fully, simply for the effect on the men." O'Neill boasted, "The Spanish bullet isn't made that will kill me." A few minutes later, he was hit in the head.

With casualties rising, it was impossible to hold the men any longer at the edge of the meadow; either they must advance or retreat. Miley sent back word from the skirmish line: "The heights must be taken at all hazards. A retreat now would be a disastrous defeat." By noon the men were advancing rapidly. Knox wrote:

"The enemy were slowly withdrawing from the brush into the bottoms of the trenches on the hills. As they withdrew, we advanced on our hands and knees, crawling on our stomachs at times, and where the ground permitted, with a rush, until we had driven them all to the hilltops. Now began the serious work of the day. We had to dislodge an enemy our equal or superior in numbers from a strongly fortified and entrenched position on the ranges of hills that surround the city."

At about one o'clock, General Sumner ordered his brigades to attack Kettle Hill.

Roosevelt paraded conspicuously in front of his men, fully exposed on horseback. When the order came to attack, he rode back and forth, assembling the regiment. He considered it too dangerous to reamin at the foot of the hill firing, so ordered his own men, accompanied by fragments of four other regiments, to charge:

"By this time we were all in the spirit of the thing and greatly excited by the charge, the men cheering and running forward between shots. . . . I . . . galloped toward the hill, passing the shouting, cheering, firing men, and went up the lane, splashing through a small stream; when I got abreast of the ranch buildings on top of Kettle Hill, I turned and went up the slope. Being on horseback I was, of course, able to get ahead of the men on

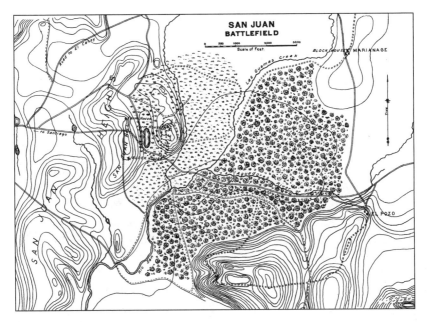

Scribner's *map of San Juan Battlefield*

Sixteenth Infantry crossing creek under fire

Wounded Spanish prisoners on San Juan Hill, July 3

foot, excepting my orderly, Henry Bardshar, who had run ahead very fast in order to get better shots at the Spaniards, who were now running out of the ranch buildings. . . . Some forty yards from the top I ran into a wire fence and jumped off Little Texas, turning him loose. He had been scraped by a couple of bullets, one of which nicked my elbow, and I never expected to see him again. As I ran up the hill, Bardshar stopped to shoot, and two Spaniards fell as he emptied his magazine. These were the only Spaniards I actually saw fall to aimed shots by any one of my men, with the exception of two guerillas in trees.

"Almost immediately afterward the hill was covered by the troops, both Rough Riders and the colored troops of the Ninth, and some men of the First. . . . One Spaniard was captured in the buildings, another was shot as he tried to hide himself, and a few others were killed as they ran.

"No sooner were we on the crest than the Spaniards from the line of hills in our front, where they were strongly intrenched, opened a very heavy fire upon us with their rifles. They also opened upon us with one or two pieces of artillery, using time fuses which burned very accurately, the shells exploding right over our heads.

"On top of the hill was a huge iron kettle, or something of the kind, probably used for sugar refining. Several of our men took shelter behind this. We had a splendid view of the charge on the San Juan block-house to our left, where the infantry of Kent, led by Hawkins, were climbing the hill."

Lieutenant John H. Parker and his detachment of Gatling machine guns prepared the way for the main charge on the San Juan blockhouse. In skirmishes against Indians on the Great Plains the machine guns with their relatively short range had been of little use. Against San Juan Hill the "coffee grinders" were as spectacularly successful as the artillery had been a failure. "The battery opened with 3 guns simultaneously at 1:15 P.M., using ranges of 600 to 800 yards," reported Parker. "The enemy at first concentrated his fire upon us, but soon weakened, and in five minutes was clambering from his trenches and running to the rear. We fired as rapidly as possible upon the groups thus presented until I saw a white handkerchief waved by someone of my own regiment, the Thirteenth Infantry, and at the same moment Captain Landis, First United States Cavalry, who had voluntarily assisted me throughout, said: 'Better stop; our own men are climbing up the ridge.' I ordered the fire to cease at 1:23½ P.M." A Spanish officer later told Parker, "It was terrible when your guns opened—always. They went b-r-r-r, like a lawn mower cutting the grass over our trenches. We could not stick a finger up when you fired without getting it cut off."

As soon as the Gatling guns opened fire, General Hawkins and Lieutenant Ord rallied the Sixth and Sixteenth Infantry to start them up the slope of San Juan Hill. General Hawkins was a commanding figure, with his white hair and beard, standing erect, swinging his hat and yelling, "Come on, come on." Richard Harding Davis, although suffering from a painful attack of sciatica, was on the skirmish line to watch them:

"I have seen many illustrations and pictures of this charge on the San Juan hills, but none of them seem to show it just as I remember it. In the picture-papers the men are running up hill swiftly and gallantly, in regular formation, rank after rank, with flags flying, their eyes aflame, and their hair streaming, their bayonets fixed, in long, brilliant lines, an invincible, overpowering weight of numbers. Instead of which I think the thing which impressed one the most, when our men started from cover, was that they were so few. It seemed as if someone had made an awful and terrible mistake. One's instinct was to call to them to come back."

"Yes, they were going up the hill, up the hill," wrote Stephen Crane. "It was the best moment of anybody's life. An officer said to me afterward: 'If we had been in that position and the Spaniards had come at us, we would have piled them up so high the last man couldn't have climbed over.' But up went the regiments with no music save that ceaseless fierce crashing of rifles.

"The foreign attachés were shocked. 'It is very gallant, but very foolish,' said one sternly.

"'Why, they can't take it, you know! Never in the world!' cried another. 'It is slaughter!'"

To some observers, the troops looked like an unfolding ribbon of blue as they moved forward. Davis wrote:

"They had no glittering bayonets, they were not massed in regular array. There were a few men in advance, bunched together, and creeping up a steep, sunny hill, the tops of which roared and flashed with flame. The men held their guns pressed across their breasts and stepped heavily as they climbed. Behind these first few, spreading out like a fan, were single lines of men, slipping and scrambling in the smooth grass, moving forward with difficulty, as though they were wading waist high through water, moving slowly, carefully, with strenuous effort. It was much more wonderful than any swinging charge could have been. They walked to greet death at every step, many of them, as they advanced, sinking suddenly or pitching forward and disappearing in the high grass, but the others waded on, stubbornly, forming a thin blue line that kept creeping higher and higher up the hill. It was inevitable as the rising tide. It was a miracle of self-sacrifice, a triumph of bull-dog courage, which one watched breathless with wonder. The fire of the Spanish riflemen, who still stuck bravely to their posts, doubled and trebled in fierceness, the crests of the hills crackled and burst in amazed roars, and rippled with waves of tiny flame. But the blue line crept steadily up and on, and then, near the top, the broken fragments gathered together with a sudden burst of speed, the Spaniards appeared for a moment outlined against the sky and poised for instant flight, fired a last volley and fled before the swift-moving wave that leaped and sprang up after them."

Casualties were relatively light going up the slope because most of the Spanish bullets went over the heads of the attacking troops, but the slaughter was not over. Lieutenant Ord led the right side of the line up the hill and leaped over the trench. Just as he jumped, he was shot fatally by a wounded Spaniard.

As the Americans made the final rush to the top of San Juan Hill, Roosevelt on Kettle Hill called to his men to charge the next line of Spanish trenches on the hills to their front, from which a damaging fire was coming:

"Thinking that the men would all come, I jumped over the wire fence in front of us and started at the double; but, as a matter of fact, the troopers were so excited, what with shooting and being shot, and shouting and cheering, that they did not hear, or did not heed me; and after running about a hundred yards I found I had only five men along with me." Two of them were wounded. Roosevelt went back, rallied the Rough Riders, who protested they had not heard him, and assembled men from other regiments.

"By this time everybody had his attention attracted," Roosevelt wrote. "The men of the various regiments which were already on the hill came with a rush, and we started across the wide valley which lay between us and the Spanish intrenchments. . . . Long before we got near them the Spaniards ran, save a few here and there, who either surrendered or were shot down. When we reached the trenches we found them filled with dead bodies in the light blue and white uniform of the Spanish regular army. . . .

"I was with Henry Bardshar, running up at the double, and two Spaniards leaped from the trenches and fired at us, not ten yards away. As they turned to run I closed in and fired twice, missing the first and killing the second. My revolver was from the sunken battleship *Maine.*

"There was very great confusion at this time, the different regiments being completely intermingled—white regulars, col-

The charge as Stoopendall imagined it

Charging up the Hill

Roosevelt and men on crest overlooking Santiago

Negro Troops

ored regulars, and Rough Riders. . . . We were still under a heavy fire, and I got together a mixed lot of men and pushed on from the trenches and ranch-houses which we had just taken, driving the Spaniards through a line of palm-trees, and over the crest of a chain of hills. When we reached these crests we found ourselves overlooking Santiago."

The fighting was still heavy as the Spaniards continued their resistance. The thin line of American troops was by no means sure it could hold its position. The correspondents trudged up San Juan Hill, past the Spanish and American dead, to obtain a closer view of the battle. "The air was absolutely crowded with Spanish bullets," Remington reported. "The shrapnel came screaming over. A ball struck in front of me, and filled my hair and face with sand, some of which I did not get out for days. It jolted my glass and my nerves, and I beat a masterly retreat, crawling rapidly backwards." But Stephen Crane paraded up and down in full sight of the Spanish riflemen, dressed in a conspicuous white raincoat. Davis wrote:

"The fire from the enemy was so heavy that only one troop along the entire line of the hills was returning it, and all the rest of our men were lying down. General Wood . . . and I were lying on our elbows at Crane's feet, and Wood ordered him also to lie down. Crane pretended not to hear, and moved farther away, still peering over the hill with the same interested expression. Wood told him for the second time that if he did not lie down he would be killed, but Crane paid no attention. So, in order to make him take shelter, I told him he was trying to impress us with his courage. . . . He dropped to his knees, as I had hoped he would, and we breathed again."

Remington, back on the San Juan road, asked a wounded man, "How goes it?"

"'Ammunition! Ammunition!' said the man, forgetful of his wound. . . .

"I again started out to the hill, along with a pack-train loaded with ammunition. A mule went down, and bullets and shell were coming over the hill aplenty. The wounded going to the rear cheered the ammunition, and when it was unpacked at the front, the soldiers seized it like gold. They lifted a box in the air and dropped it on one corner, which smashed it open.

"'Now we can hold San Juan hill against them garlics—hey, son!' yelled a happy cavalryman to a doughboy."

Hold they did, until the sun went down, wearily preparing to stand off further attacks. There was little firing after 4:30, but General Shafter was alarmed by the precarious position of his thin line of troops. Over a thousand of them had been killed or wounded. There was no reserve, so that the exhausted survivors had to hold on by themselves until Lawton's even more exhausted troops could arrive after an all-night march from El Caney. The Americans had triumphed by such a meager margin that on the night of July 1 they could not see the dimensions of their victory—only the imminence of disaster.

The immediate result of the battle among the survivors had been to help erase lines of section and color. Frank Knox wrote home that he had become separated from the Rough Riders, "but I joined a troop of the Tenth Cavalry, colored, and for a time fought with them shoulder to shoulder, and in justice to the colored race I must say that I never saw braver men anywhere. Some of those who rushed up the hill will live in my memory forever."

Lieutenant Pershing felt that a new unity had come out of the trial by battle: "White regiments, black regiments, regulars and Rough Riders, representing the young manhood of the North and the South, fought shoulder to shoulder, unmindful of race or color, unmindful of whether commanded by an ex-Confederate or not, and mindful only of their common duty as Americans."

10

A Precarious Toehold

We at within measurable distance of a terrible military disaster," warned Theodore Roosevelt two days after the charge up San Juan Hill. As serious fighting continued, the Americans seemed to be maintaining no more than a toehold on the crests of the ridges overlooking Santiago, and seriously feared that momentarily they might be thrown back.

For most of the men who had fought their way up to the Spanish blockhouses on July 1, there was no thought except to hold, but some of the officers worried over the weakness of the long line. In the afternoon, General Shafter ordered "Fighting Joe" Wheeler, who had resumed command of the Cavalry Division, "Hold the ground where you are until night, keeping under the hill where entrenching tools will be sent to the front as soon as it is dark. Rations and artillery will be sent also."

Wheeler agreed that fortifying the ridge was of prime importance. "If we get this work well forward to-night," he replied at 5:45, "we can continue it to-morrow and the men can have comparative security." At 8:20 he reported:

"I examined the line in front of Wood's Brigade and gave the men shovels and picks and insisted on their going right to work. I also sent word to General Kent . . . and saw General Hawkins. . . . They all promise to do their best, but say the earth is very difficult, as a great part of it is rocky. . . .

"A number of officers have appealed to me to have the line withdrawn and take up a strong position farther back, and I expect they will appeal to you. I have positively discountenanced this, as it would cost us much prestige.

"Our lines are now very thin, as so many of the men have gone to the rear with the wounded, and so many are exhausted; but I hope these men can be got up to-night, and with our line intrenched and Lawton on our right we ought to hold to-morrow, but I fear it will be a severe day. If we can get through to-morrow all right, we can make our breastworks very strong the next night. You can hardly realize the exhausted condition of the troops. The 3d and 6th Cavalry and other troops were up marching and halted on the road all last night, and have fought for twelve hours to-day, and those that are not on the line will be digging trenches to-night.

"I was on the extreme front line. The men were lying down and reported the Spaniards not more than three hundred yards in their front."

The consensus, Lieutenant Pershing later declared, was that "we can hold this line against the whole Spanish army":

"Weak parts of the line were strengthened by new dispositions of troops; after dark lines of siege intrenchments were laid out; picks and shovels were brought up; companies to dig and others to guard them were designated; the night was spent in digging and men sprang to arms only when interrupted by Spanish volleys or by annoying sharpshooters.

"There was but little sleep that night; many men, even those who had opportunity, forgot to eat, and all thought of water as a luxury; ambulances and even wagons were pressed into service and kept busy until dawn gathering up the wounded; only a few of the dead were buried; pack trains carried ammunition instead of commissaries. By morning the position was strengthened so that our line was fairly well protected; reveille was sounded by Spanish small arms and artillery in chorus, but the signal had been anticipated and all men were in their places on the firing line."

The artillery was ready too. It had moved to the front line in the night, only five hundred yards from the Spanish infantry trenches, and, it turned out in the morning, in plain view. The artillerymen worked hard, but by daybreak had excavated pits only about a foot deep in the rocky ground. Lieutenant Aultman reminisced:

"At daybreak the order was received 'to bombard Santiago' and, as there was a thin mist overhanging in our entire front, through which nothing could be distinctly observed, there was nothing else to do but cock the guns up to a convenient angle, point them in the direction of the city and open fire. No objectives were visible, and none was prescribed, nor was there a mission of any kind assigned to the batteries. Merely another commentary upon our military preparedness and efficiency.

"The reply was immediate and emphatic. The great clouds of white smoke from our obsolete powder hung over the batteries and, while obscuring everything from us, rendered our position beautifully visible to the Infantry and Artillery of the enemy. The crash of rifle fire from our immediate front commenced almost instantly, with the continuous whine of bullets through our positions and the sharp cracking sound when they struck wood or metal on the guns and carriages. The Artillery fire of the enemy was not long delayed and very soon shrapnel and shells were adding their share to our discomfiture. The men, absolutely in the open and for the first time under fire, at once took refuge in the trenches of the captured position . . . and our firing ceased. Only with time and effort could the gun detachments be collected and driven back to the guns . . . and . . . a desultory fire was again opened, the usual target being the vacant world in front, though as quickly as the source of enemy fire could be recognized from the trenches in front, the guns were roughly pointed in that direction, loaded with canister or shrapnel cut at zero and fired point blank."

The army withdrew the artillery to El Pozo.

The firing was heavy throughout the day. The Spaniards did not attack the Americans, but neither did the Americans dare charge the Spanish positions, which were far stronger and more heavily defended than those on San Juan Hill had been. For the tired men in the trenches, it was a miserable day. General Hawkins was wounded, and casualties were heavy. Trooper Frank Knox of the Rough Riders wrote home:

"I spent most of the night digging trenches. After the last relief I lay down under a little tree and slept until early dawn, when I was awakened from a deep sleep by a volley from the enemy. To the time of whistling bullets we danced for the trenches. Once there, we were safe, so long as we kept under cover.

"If any one has discovered a more uncomfortable place to spend a hot day than in a four foot trench, I have yet to hear of it. Oh, the misery of those ten hours I put in there I shall never forget. One had to sit all cramped up with no opportunity to move; just sit there and fry and boil and sweat under the blistering sun and drink muddy water and chew an occasional hardtack.

"About 1 o'clock our relief came out from behind the brow of the hill. They had to rush across an open space exposed to the fire of the enemy and then lay down beside the trenches. Then we crawled out and they crawled in. And then we made our run. When I reached the other side of the hill I was so weak I could hardly stand. We got some hot coffee and warm food, and then I went to sleep. Don't imagine now that behind that hill was a place of safety. Every once in a while a shell would drop over among us and get a few of us. Then as we lay we were exposed to the return fire from our trenches on our right which made an angle with the trenches we had dug. However, there was no choice in the matter, so we laid there and slept and ate and lived . . . regularly taking our turns in the trenches."

For the wounded, the suffering was interminable. Those that managed to arrive alive at Siboney were relatively well off. George Kennan of the Red Cross found the hospital there in relatively good working order:

"As fast as the wounded arrived, they walked, or were carried on stretchers, to two or three large tents, pitched end to end and opening into one another, where hospital stewards and nurses placed them on tables, and the surgeons, some of them stripped naked to the waist, examined their injuries by candlelight, and performed such operations as were necessary to give them relief. They were then taken or led away, and as far as possible, furnished with blankets and shelter. . . . The wounded who came in after midnight were laid in a row on the ground and covered with a long strip of canvas."

But at the First Division field hospital in a glade near the Aguadores River, Kennan found an appalling lack of supplies, only two ambulances operating, and tent shelter for only about a hundred wounded men:

"The small force of field-surgeons worked heroically and with a devotion that I have never seen surpassed; but they were completely overwhelmed by the great bloody wave of human agony that rolled back in ever-increasing volume from the battle-line. They stood at the operating-tables, wholly without sleep, and almost without rest or food, for twenty-one consecutive hours; and yet, in spite of their tremendous exertions, hundreds of seriously or dangerously wounded men lay on the ground for hours, many of them half naked, and nearly all without shelter from the blazing tropical sun in the daytime, or the damp, chilly dew at night. No organized or systematic provision had been made for feeding them or giving them drink, and many a poor fellow had not tasted food or water for twelve hours. . . .

"The tents set apart for wounded soldiers were already full to overflowing, and all that a litter-squad could do with a man when they lifted him from the operating-table on Friday night was to carry him away and lay him down, half naked as he was, on the water-soaked ground under the stars. Weak and shaken from agony under the surgeon's knife and probe, there he had to lie in the high, wet grass, with no one to look after him. . . .

"The scenes of Saturday were like those of the previous day, but with added details of misery and horror. Many of the wounded, brought in from the extreme right flank of the army at Caney, had had nothing to eat or drink in more than twenty-four hours, and were in a state of extreme exhaustion. . . .

"At midnight Saturday the number of wounded men that had been brought into the hospital camp was about eight hundred. All that could walk, after their wounds had been dressed, and all that could bear transportation to the seacoast in an army wagon, were sent to Siboney to be put on board the hospital steamers and transports. There remained in camp several hundred who were so severely injured that they could not possibly be moved, and these were carried to the eastern end of the field and laid on the ground in the high, wet grass. . . .

"On Saturday afternoon I telephoned Miss [Clara] Barton from General Shafter's headquarters to send us blankets, clothing, malted milk, beef extract, tents, tent-flies, and such other things as were most urgently needed. Sunday afternoon, less than twenty-four hours after my message reached her, she rode into the hospital camp in an army wagon . . . with . . . everything necessary for a small Red Cross emergency station, and in less than two hours they were refreshing all the wounded men in the camp with corn-meal gruel, hot malted milk, beef extract, coffee, and a beverage known as 'Red Cross cider.' . . . After that time no sick or wounded man in the camp, I think, ever suffered for want of suitable food and drink. . . .

"In spite of unfavorable conditions, the percentage of recoveries among the wounded treated in this hospital was much greater than in any other war in which the United States has ever been engaged. This was due partly to improved antiseptic methods of treatment, and partly to the [small, clean] wounds made by the Mauser bullet. . . . All abdominal operations that were attempted in the field resulted in death, and none were performed after the first day, as the great heat and dampness, together with the difficulty of giving the patients proper nursing and care, made recovery next to impossible."

One of the wounded men able to make his way back to Siboney was Trooper Arthur Fortunatus Cosby. In a dispatch to *Harper's Weekly*, John Fox, Jr., referred to him as "That wounded courtier . . . who, feverish, trembling, with a scraped temple, a badly wounded hand, and a bullet in his chest, staggered painfully some ten miles, waving off all assistance, and confessing at last, as he sat on the beach, in the broiling sun, waiting to be taken to a hospital-ship, that if it were handy, and could be got without too much trouble, he thought he would like a peach."

To another correspondent, Cosby dictated a letter for his mother: "I have been in another engagement & am slightly wounded—not seriously. I was lying in the grass, storming an intrenched blockhouse near Santiago, when a ball entered my hat, grazed my temple, went through the fleshy part of my hand in 3 places, & lodged in the muscles of the right chest. . . . I am not suffering at all."

Ten days later, on July 12, Cosby again had his picture taken at the same Tampa studio where he had been photographed on June 6.

Trooper Cosby was indeed relatively lucky. Some of the men with whom he had fought the day before were being buried in the Spanish trenches on San Juan Hill. Along the road stretching back to El Pozo, Caspar Whitney saw many grim sights in the gray dawn of July 2:

"Dead men lying beside the road, ghastly in their unstudied positions; men dying, men wounded, passing back to the division hospital, some being carried, some limping, some sitting by the road-side, all strangely silent, bandaged and bloody. Beyond the second crossing the road was strewn with parts of clothes, blanket-rolls, cups, pieces of bacon, empty cans, cartridges; at the forks the marks of bullets were everywhere—the trees shot through and through. There were plenty of live bullets coming over the ridge that morning too."

One of the wounded officers, Captain John Bigelow, Jr., of the Tenth Cavalry, had been painfully jarred and jolted in an army wagon that hauled him the nine miles into Siboney. Nevertheless, he could feel compassion for a group of Spanish prisoners that were being marched in:

"Like Cubans, they were small, lightly built men. They marched at a good gait, keeping up with the long-legged horses of their escort. . . . They bore themselves, I thought, with true Spanish dignity, holding their heads high even when glancing to right or left at the staring crowd. Cuban women hung over the railing of the porches pointing and jeering at them. The Cuban men watched them with comparative gravity."

During the second of July, the Americans greatly strengthened their lines. Lawton's men, after marching heroically most of the night, from El Caney by way of El Pozo, reinforced and extended the right wing. The Ninth Massachusetts and Thirty-fourth Michigan regiments hastily disembarked and rushed to

Arthur F. Cosby, July 12, 1898

Under heavy fire, in improved trenches

Santiago from the heights

the front. The Thirty-third Michigan, as it had the day before, feinted against Spanish troops guarding a bridge at the mouth of the Aguadores River; in an emergency it too could have hurried to the front. Shafter's adjutant, McClernand, reviewing the campaign years later, concluded:

"With all the additional troops added on the second [of July] to those who fought victoriously at San Juan the day before, there should have been no doubt in the mind of any one about our ultimate success, and there would not have been except for the fact that our Army was tired, very tired. Its wonderful burst of speed was followed by great physical weariness, but it would have been well for all to have recalled that the enemy had been beaten and driven back everywhere, and certainly must have been greatly discouraged."

American casualties had been frighteningly large. By the next morning, July 3, they had lost 143 killed and 1,010 wounded, in addition to the casualties at El Caney. Roosevelt warned Lodge that disaster impended:

"Tell the President for Heaven's sake to send us every regiment and above all every battery possible. We have won so far at a heavy cost, but the Spaniards fight very hard and charging these intrenchments against modern rifles is terrible. . . . We *must* have help—thousands of men, batteries, and *food* and ammunition."

Although the firing had diminished during the previous afternoon of July 2, many of the officers became so alarmed over the weakness of the American position that they strongly recommended falling back. McClernand was shocked to find that a pack train loaded with ammunition bound for the front had instead been ordered to unload at El Pozo. He ordered it reloaded and taken forward, then, troubled, went to headquarters:

"That evening about dusk the division commanders and General Bates . . . reported at Battle Headquarters . . . [to]

General Shafter. . . . He was still ill and so weak that a door was taken from its hinges and placed for him to recline upon. His pluck at being there at all was so manifest that all present admired it. Besides those mentioned several staff officers, including myself, attended the Council of War. . . . It was held in the open and sentinels were posted to keep all except those authorized to be there at a distance."

Shafter "opened the discussion by saying, in substance, that it had been represented to him that he had pushed the Army too far to the front, and that if this could be shown to be the case he would withdraw some distance until better preparations could be made to capture the city. He then called for an expression of opinions. Conflicting views were given . . . finally the Commanding General said, in effect: "Well, gentlemen; it is possible I have gotten you too far to the front, but I have always thought I had the courage to admit an error if I made one, and if we fall back I will take all blame . . . unless, however, you get orders to the contrary you will hold your positions.' . . .

"The Council broke up and each officer started for his proper post. . . .

"Suddenly a terrific roar of musketry burst upon the stillness of the night. . . . Apparently every man in the two armies who was armed with a rifle was engaged in 'rapid fire.' It seemed as if the inferno had broken loose. Some of our people thought the Spaniards were trying to cut their way out, and later we learned they thought we were trying to break in. The din was doubtless started by a few tired men nervous because they were tired."

A Rough Rider lieutenant a few weeks later told Ray Stannard Baker that at the height of the fusillade, when he thought he saw the Spaniards "in a dense dark line at the top of the hill": "For a moment the men in the trenches stirred restlessly, and then they saw Colonel Roosevelt walking calmly along the top of the entrenchment with a faded blue handkerchief flapping from the back of his hat, wholly unmindful of the bullets which hummed about him like a hive of bees. A cheer went up, and calls for the Colonel to come down, and that was the end of the restlessness."

Roosevelt described the incident in a matter-of-fact way. The Spaniards had suddenly attacked one of his pickets, wounding him seriously. This sputter of fire led to heavy firing on both sides, and word went to the commanders that the Spaniards were attacking:

"It was imperative to see what was really going on, so I ran up to the trenches and looked out. At night it was far easier to place the Spanish lines than by day, because the flame-spurts shone in the darkness. I could soon tell that there were bodies of Spanish pickets or skirmishers in the jungle-covered valley, between their lines and ours, but that the bulk of the fire came from their trenches and showed not the slightest symptom of advancing; moreover, as is generally the case at night, the fire was almost all high, passing well overhead, with an occasional bullet near by. . . . Soon we got the troopers in hand, and made them cease firing; then, after a while the Spanish fire died down. . . .

"That night we spent in perfecting the trenches and arranging entrances to them, doing about as much work as we had the preceding night. . . . Next morning, at daybreak, the firing began again. This day, the 3d, we suffered nothing, save having one man wounded by a sharpshooter, and, thanks to the approaches of the trenches, we were able to relieve the guards without any difficulty."

The battle had simmered down into a state of siege. Shafter was extending his lines around Santiago as rapidly as possible, but not in time to prevent the entrance on July 3 of Colonel Federico Escario with thirty-six hundred Spanish troops. They successfully eluded General García's Cuban force which had been assigned to block them. Even with reinforcements, the Spanish were too weak to breach the American lines, and the siege lines had cut off their supplies of water and fresh food.

Shafter worried nevertheless over the predictions of his more pessimistic commanders that Spanish artillery could rake some of the American trenches, and that the heavy rains would prevent bringing supplies from the beachhead.

In Washington, President McKinley and his secretary of war were worried also, as no report came from Shafter. On the morning of July 3, Alger cabled Shafter:

"I waited with the President until 4 o'clock this morning for news from you relative to Saturday's battle. Not a word was received, nor has there been up to this hour, 11 A.M. . . . I wish hereafter that you would interrupt all messages that are being sent to the Associated Press and others, and make report at the close of each day."

In a few minutes they received a most unsettling message from Shafter:

"We have the town well invested on the north and east, but with a very thin line. Upon approaching it we find it of such a character and defenses so strong it will be impossible to carry it by storm with my present force, and I am seriously considering withdrawing about 5 miles."

At once Alger replied: "Of course you can judge the situation better than we can at this end of the line. If, however, you could hold your present position, especially San Juan heights, the effect upon the country would be much better than falling back."

At the same time that Shafter prepared for a possible withdrawal, he undertook the bold expedient of demanding the surrender of Santiago. According to Miley, he had decided upon it during the night. McClernand years later reminisced:

"Early the next morning, July 3, my chief sent for me and said he wished to cable Washington. He dictated and I took down his words. . . . I felt confident that with a little rest no one in the Army would care to fall back, and had emphatically expressed the opinion the night before that all we had to do was to hold on and the ripening fruit would fall into our hands. . . . Returning to [Shafter about an hour later], I said: 'General, let us make a demand on them to surrender.' He was still ill and lying on his cot. He looked at me for perhaps a full minute and I thought he was going to offer a rebuke for my persistence in opposing those who had advised withdrawal, but finally he said: 'Well, try it.' I went under a tent fly that served for my office and wrote the demand of 8:30 A.M."

It read: "I shall be obliged, unless you surrender, to shell Santiago de Cuba. Please inform the citizens of foreign countries, and all women and children, that they should leave the city before 10 o'clock to-morrow morning.

"Very respectfully, your obedient servant,

WILLIAM R. SHAFTER
Major-General, U.S.V."

11

The Fleet
Darts Out

If I were to live a thousand years and a thousand centuries never should I forget that 3d day of July, 1898, nor do I believe that Spain will ever forget it," wrote Lieutenant José Müller y Tejeiro of the Spanish navy. Neither would General Shafter, agonizing with indecision at his headquarters, nor Admiral Sampson, preparing to come ashore to confer with him. Nor would the American people, for whom the day won the war but helped create a diplomatic revolution, bringing an inexorable involvement in world politics. July 3, 1898, was one of the most momentous days in the history of the United States.

It started out as a peaceful Sunday morning. There would be quarters, inspection, and religious services which would relieve somewhat the growing tedium aboard the blockading vessels. After the weeks of strain guarding the mouth of Santiago harbor, no one really expected the Spanish fleet to come out. Certainly Admiral Sampson did not. He had sent the battleship *Massachusetts* and the *Suwanee* to Guantánamo to refuel, and that morning further weakened his blockading forces by sailing to Daiquiri aboard the relatively speedy *New York,* accompanied by the *Hist* and the *Ericsson.*

Admiral Sampson left behind him in an arc of about eight miles' radius, centering on the harbor mouth, the armed yachts *Vixen* and *Gloucester,* the cruiser *Brooklyn,* and the battleships *Oregon, Iowa,* and *Texas.* The tide had swept the vessels somewhat out of position; on the eastern side of the arc there were large gaps on each side of the *Brooklyn.* Several of the vessels, to economize on coal, had unhooked several of their engines, which seriously cut their speed. It would take much time to fire the cold boilers, and twenty minutes standing still to couple the engines to the drive shaft. Fortunately, the *Oregon* at least had steam in all of her boilers. This was an incredible economy—and a needless one, since plenty of coal was available—in facing a fleet reputedly faster. Otherwise, the American fleet was completely ready.

"Battle-hatches were off temporarily, to give what little relief was possible to the sweltering crews," wrote Captain Robley D. Evans of the *Iowa;* "electric-firing batteries and ammunition-hoists had been carefully examined. . . .

"I had just finished my breakfast, and was sitting smoking at my cabin table, in conversation with my son, a naval cadet. . . . At thirty-one minutes after nine o'clock the general alarm for action rang all over the ship. My son jumped to his feet, exclaiming, 'Papa, the enemy's ships are coming out!' and we both started as fast as we could go for the bridge. Before I had reached the spar-deck I heard a gun fired from the *Iowa,* and upon reaching the bridge found the signal flying. . . . The engine-gongs rang, 'Full speed ahead,' and the *Iowa* closed in as she slowly gathered speed. At this moment the Spanish cruiser *Infanta María Teresa* was in plain view, coming around Smith Cay in front of the Punta Gorda battery, her magnificent battle-flag just showing clear of the land as I reached the bridge."

Aboard the *María Teresa*, Captain Victor M. Concas y Palau asked permission of Admiral Cervera to open fire; receiving it, he ordered bugles blown to signal the beginning of the battle:

"The sound of my bugles was the last echo of those which history tells us were sounded at the capture of Granada. It was the signal that the history of four centuries of grandeur was at an end and that Spain was becoming a nation of the fourth class.

"'Poor Spain!' I said to my noble and beloved admiral, and he answered by an expressive motion, as though to say that he had done everything possible to avoid it, and that his conscience was clear. And this was true."

Admiral Cervera was standing in the forward tower beside the pilot, Miguel López, as they emerged from the harbor mouth. "By this time there were already many dead and wounded in the battery, because they had been firing on us for some time," López later declared. "The Admiral said to me:

"'Good-by, pilot; go now; go, and be sure you let them pay you, because you have earned it well.'"

Fatalistically, Admiral Cervera, who had opposed bringing the squadron to the New World, had accepted orders to take it out to what he and his captains were certain would be sudden destruction. The bottoms of his vessels were foul, drastically cutting their speed. An estimated 85 per cent of the ammunition was defective and worthless; the fastest vessel, the *Colón*, lacked heavy armament. Worst of all, the vessels were decked and ornamented with wood, which as far as possible should have been ripped out while they were in harbor.

Yet their plight was not helpless. Governor-General Blanco had urged Cervera to take them out at night—and it had been the constant worry of the blockading forces that they would emerge during a squall some night. But Cervera feared that the blinding rays of the searchlights focused on the harbor entrance would make it impossible for the pilots to guide his squadron through the treacherous channel, avoiding the hulk of the *Merrimac*. Even in the daytime, American naval officers later thought, part of the squadron should have escaped had it scattered and headed for open sea.

Rather, Cervera, although singularly brave, pursued a more cautious course. He ordered the entire squadron to swing to the east together, where little but the cruiser *Brooklyn*, their fastest opponent, blocked them. They would attract the concentrated fire of the blockading fleet by steaming as a unit, but some vessels might be successful in reaching Cienfuegos or Havana. If they failed, they could beach their vessels rather than having them sink with all their men in deep water. Cervera's strategy was more humane than daring.

The American plan of attack as laid down by Admiral Sampson in advance was singularly simple—and unworkable: converge upon the Spanish ships to destroy them at the mouth of the harbor. It was impossible, because although the Spanish squadron was emerging slowly, dropping the pilots one by one and making way at no more than five or six knots, the American vessels, riding on the roadstead, took several minutes to get under way, and additional minutes to close in. To the men aboard the battleships, as Captain Henry C. Taylor of the *Indiana* remembered, it seemed an eternity:

"The length of time . . . was not . . . two minutes from the time of the first signal until the *Indiana's* engines were turning over and the guns trained upon the Morro . . . but the impatience of all hands made it seem much longer. . . . Lieuenant Henderson, commanding the powder division, whose men, in getting below to their stations, were obliged to pass through one or two narrow hatches, or scuttles, told me that it seemed and hour to him getting his one hundred and seventy-two men below to their stations, but that it was really less than two minutes. To hurry them he shouted, 'They will all get away; two of them are outside the

Morro already!' at which, desperate at the thought of such a thing, his men simply 'fell below,' throwing themselves down the steep ladder in their eagerness to reach their posts, until the ammunition-deck was swarming with bruised and bleeding men, staggering to their feet, and limping to their stations."

The rush at the Spanish ships, which might have involved collisions in the clouds of gunsmoke, turned fortunately into a chase. Since Admiral Sampson was away, Commodore Schley assumed command, but it was, as Roosevelt later declared (with San Juan Hill in mind), a battle of the captains. It was also, with the ships firing at each other at close range, a re-markable spectacle.

"The Spanish ships came out as gaily as brides to the altar," Captain John W. Philip of the *Texas* wrote. "Handsome vessels they certainly were, and with flags enough flying for a cele-bration parade. . . . Just as I reached the bridge the foremost of the advancing Spanish ships poked her nose around Puntilla. As she swung around, she fired, and almost immediately after-ward our forward six-inch spoke. The first shell fired by Cervera threw up a column of water short of us and between the *Texas* and the *Iowa*.

"On each side of the *Texas* the *Brooklyn* and the *Iowa* were coming up with a tremendous rush. The dash of these two ships, as soon as the alarm was given, straight for the enemy, with cas-cades of water pouring away from their bows (the proverbial 'bone in her teeth' of the writers on nautical matters), was one of the most beautiful sights of the battle. They seemed to me to spring forward as a hound from the leash. Farther east, the *Oregon* and the *Indiana* were also headed in, ready for business."

Commodore Schley had rushed to a little platform he had had constructed around the conning tower of the *Brooklyn*; Captain Francis A. Cook joined him. The navigator, Lieutenant Albon C. Hodgson, sang out to Schley, "Commodore, they are coming right at us." "Well," Schley replied, "go right for them."

"The *Brooklyn*, as well as the other vessels of the squadron, charged immediately in to the entrance, in accordance with the original plan," Schley later testified.

"We continued on this course, porting and starboarding, to meet the movement of the leading ship . . . we were ten to twelve minutes turning; first with port helm, and then advancing directly towards the enemy. I saw the ships to the eastward and westward [of the entrance] closing in.

"I said to Captain Cook: "Close action," or "Close up" has been hoisted; and it means to keep about a thousand yards away, so as to be out of their effective torpedo range.

"'Much will depend upon this ship this day.'

"Captain Cook was standing close alongside of me. He said: 'Yes, we will soon be within the cross-fire of these ships.' I said, 'Yes.' We had advanced and were firing. . . .

"I saw the leading [Spanish] ship, which apparently had started with the intention of ramming, take a most decided sheer to the westward, leaving a gap between her and the ship following . . . the *Vizcaya*. We were standing in the direction of the *Vizcaya*, when she also . . . turned . . . to the westward. . . .

"It then became apparent, as we were steering on diametrically opposite courses, that the original plan had failed; and that the Spanish fleet in order, and apparently at distance [about four hundred yards apart], had succeeded in passing the battleship line."

As for Captain Concas, lamenting the passing of Spain's centuries-old glory:

"The second gun of the deck battery was the first to open fire and brought us back to this reality, too dreadful to allow us to think of other things. Giving the cruiser [*Infanta María Teresa*] all her speed, we poured out a frantic fire with out whole battery, except the forward gun, which we reserved to fire at close quarters. In compliance with the order received, I put our bow toward the armored cruiser *Brooklyn*, which, putting to starboard, presented her stern to us and fired her two after turret guns, moving to southward. . . . The position of the *Brooklyn*, and the fact of her being close to the others, which advanced as she receded, cause the *Texas* and *Iowa* to come between the *Teresa* and the *Brooklyn;* for this reason, as to keep on this course would have been to run the danger of being rammed by these two ships, the admiral consulted me, and we agreed that it was impossible to continue, so he ordered me to put her prow toward the coast. At that time the *Brooklyn* was about 5,416 yards and the *Texas* and *Iowa* about 3,250 yards from us.

"Behind the *Teresa* came the *Vizcaya,* followed by the *Colón,* and then the *Oquendo;* but after the *Teresa* came out of the harbor she was entirely alone for about ten minutes, during which time she had to suffer the fire of all the batteries of the enemy. This formed . . . the peculiar nature of that battle; that is to say, the American squadron was exposed to two guns of the *Teresa,* but she to all the guns of the enemy.

"The *Vizcaya* and the *Colón* came out quite close to each other, increasing, consequently, the distance between them and the *Oquendo;* and as the enemy's ships continued to pick out the admiral's ship for their fire, and especially as our other ships had orders to follow inside, they were beyond the range of the 6 pounder rapid fire guns, so that in the beginning they suffered but little; and if their engines had been in good condition and the *Vizcaya's* bottom clean, they would have been able to make a much longer resistance."

The Spanish fleet managed thus to emerge from Santiago harbor without suffering important damage, and to break past the converging American ships. Commodore Schley had to act instantly.

There followed the controversial move of the battle. The *Brooklyn,* heading toward the Spanish vessels coming from the opposite direction, had to turn, and turned in a great circle away from them—a loop that would head the *Brooklyn* to the west so it could continue the chase. Schley testified:

"Immediately Cook gave the order to port the helm. I did not. I should have done it in a second. . . . I have never seen a ship turn more rapidly than she did; and her turn was absolutely continuous; there was no easing of her helm."

At the time the turn began the closest Spanish ship was only eleven hundred yards away, Schley testified, so near "that I could see, with the naked eye, men running from her turret to her superstructure deck; and I observed daylight between their legs, as they ran. . . .

"I never saw the starboard side of the *Texas* as all. I only saw her port side, and she never approached any position that was within six hundred yards of the *Brooklyn*. She was so distant that she never entered my head as a menace or danger. . . . During the turn Mr. Hodgson (the navigator) very properly made some allusion to look out, perhaps for the *Texas*."

As for the *Texas*, Captain Philip recalled:

"The smoke from our guns began to hang so heavily and densely over the ship that for a few minutes we could see nothing. We might as well have had a blanket tied over our heads. Suddenly a whiff of breeze and a lull in the firing lifted the pall, and there, bearing toward us and across our bows, turning on her port helm, with big waves curling over her bows and great clouds of black smoke pouring from her funnels, was the *Brooklyn*. She looked as big as half a dozen *Great Easterns*, and seemed so near that it took our breath away.

"'Back both engines hard!' went down the tube to the astonished engineers, and in a twinkling the old ship was racing against herself. The collision which seemed imminent, even if it was not, was averted, and as the big cruiser glided past, all of us on the bridge gave a sigh of relief. Had the *Brooklyn* struck us then, it would probably have been an end of the *Texas* and her half-thousand men."

As the *Brooklyn* turned, Schley testified, "all four of the Spanish ships and the fort were firing at the same time. . . .

From that moment, the next ten or fifteen minutes was the most furious part of the entire combat. I remember very distinctly seeing . . . the jets of water ahead and astern; and over and short; and the roar of the projectiles was one of the things that can be heard once in a lifetime. . . .

"It appeared to me . . . that all four of those ships were at work on the *Brooklyn*; and up to that moment . . . so far as we could perceive, there was not the slightest evidence that they had been even injured.

"The thought passed through my mind that after all our precautions and waiting, those fellows would get away."

The four Spanish ships, "heading in a column to the westward, presented the finest spectacle that has probably ever been seen on the water," wrote "Fighting bob" Evans of the *Iowa*:

"Their broadsides came with mechanical rapidity, and in striking contrast to the deliberate fire of the American ships. A torrent of projectiles was sailing over us, harmlessly exploding in the water beyond. . . .

"The speed of the enemy's ships we estimated at this time to be about thirteen knots, and it was soon evident to me that I could not ram either the first or the second ship, which, up to this time, it had been my intention to do. I therefore put my helm hard astarboard, swung off to port, and gave the *Teresa* my entire broadside at a range of twenty-five hundred yards. Then, quickly shifting my helm to port, I again headed in, keeping the second ship of the enemy open on my starboard bow. The forward eight-inch guns of the port battery now opened on the *Teresa*, and my starboard battery kept firing at the *Vizcaya* and the *Almirante Oquendo*. As the *Vizcaya* ranged up ahead of me, my helm was again put hard astarboard, and she received the benefit of my starboard broadside. Again I swung back with the port helm, and laid the *Iowa* to cross the bows of the *Oquendo*. I soon found, however, that the best speed I could get out of my good ship was ten knots, and that the *Oquendo* would pass me at a range of about sixteen hundred yards. I therefore put my helm to starboard and laid a course parallel to that steered by her. At this time she was about abeam of me. Orders were given to man the rapid-fire battery, and every gun on the starboard side roared and barked at the unfortunate Spanish ship. The *Indiana* was lying on her quarter, pounding away at her, and the *Oregon* was giving her at the same time a dose on her port bow."

"The *Indiana* was, in fact, upon the flank of the Spanish column as it emerged," wrote Captain Henry C. Taylor, "and the effect of its fire was marked. One of our heavy shells struck the *Teresa* early in the action and exploded, doing great damage. Another hit the *Vizcaya* abaft the funnels, and its explosion was followed by a burst of flame which for a moment obscured the after-part of that vessel. The *Colón* and the *Oquendo*, as soon as they were clear of Morro point, fired their first broadsides, apparantly at the *Indiana* and the *Iowa*, both of which vessels replied vigorously and with excellent effect."

Meanwhile, the Spanish ships were keeping up a brisk though inaccurate fire, Taylor remembered: "Their energy, if not their skill, was commendable. We had a great advantage over them as to range: it had been our daily, hourly habit for many weeks to estimate our distance from the Morro by the eye and verify it with our sextants and stadiometers; and in emerging from the narrow entrance the Spanish ships almost touched the Morro, so that in the first few minutes, which were, in fact, the deciding moments of the battle, we had their range absolutely. . . ."

The Spanish ships "fired high at first. I could hear, from the *Indiana's* bridge, the screech and hum of many shells passing over our heads from the *Teresa* and the *Vizcaya* as they poured in their first broad-sides; and as their consorts engaged and added their fire, the sound became continuous and gradually closer to our ears and louder, as they slowly—all too slowly for their own good—corrected their range and reduced the elevation of their guns."

Because of the clouds of smoke, it was hard at times to tell just what was going on. Captain Philip of the *Texas* wrote:

"It got in our ears, noses, and mouths, blackened our faces, and blinded our eyes. Often for minutes at a time, for all we could see, we might as well have been down in the double bottoms as on the bridge. One had the sensation of standing up against an unseen foe, the most disagreeable sensation in warfare.

"As the shells were screaming about our ears in uncomfortable frequency, I decided—for the sake of the men exposed with me on the flying bridge, as well as for myself—to go to the lower bridge, which encircled the conning-tower. . . . Within a minute—in fact, while we were still on the bridge, making our way down the only ladder—a shell struck the jamb of the starboard door of the pilothouse, and exploded inside. . . .

"The *Texas* fired from her main battery only when a good target could be plainly seen. I gave explicit orders to that effect. . . . When the smoke lifted and the enemy could be seen, the gunners took careful aim and fired deliberately. . . . The men in the *Texas* turrets have reason to congratulate themselves on the fact that the two big shells which did find their way into the Spanish vessels, so far as discovered by the official board of survey, were twelve-inch shells. . . .

"In the course of our fight with the *Oquendo* a shell exploded over our forward superstructure. The concussion lifted the bridge contingent off their feet. I remember pitching up in the air, with my coat-tails flying out behind me, as if I had been thrown by one of Roosevelt's broncos. No one was hurt except Cadet Reynolds, one of whose ear-drums was split. . . .

"A few moments later the Spaniards got in a luckier shot. A shell about six inches in diameter struck forward of the ash-hoist, and, after passing through the outer plating of hammock-berthing, exploded, the mass of pieces penetrating the bulkhead and casing of the starboard smoke-pipe. This shot, fortunately, hurt nobody, but it caused considerable excitement in the fire-

room. Fragments of the shell dropped down there; the ham-
mocks and portions of the sailors' clothing stored in the
berthing caught fire and also fell below, causing such a gush of
smoke in the fire-room that some of the men thought the ship
had blown up. That there was no panic there, nor anything like
one, speaks volumes for the discipline of the men and the effi-
cieny of the engineer officers."

Meanwhile, Lieutenant Commander Richard Wainwright
had been building the steam pressure in the boilers of the
Gloucester (in peacetime J. P. Morgan's yacht *Corsair*). Although
the *Gloucester* was without armor, its task was to intercept the two
Spanish destroyers when they emerged from the harbor, to prevent them from torpedoing the battleships. "At last the destroyers made their appearance," wrote Wainwright, "and we rushed
ahead at full speed, with all the effect of the bottled-up steam.

"As we neared the destroyers, the shot and shell began to
whistle about us in a lively fashion. I can remember my astonishment at not seeing any wounded or sign of blood when I
looked about the decks. The shell from the batteries on shore
also fell about us. A shot from any one of them would have
ended our usefulness."

The officers of the *Gloucester* were not aware of it at the
time, but they were the most seriously menaced by the heavy
guns of the American battleships. Captain Taylor of the
Indiana later wrote: "My attention naturally . . . could be given
only slightly to anything else than the handling of my own
ship and its battery, and the observation of the vessels near
us. . . . Wainwright, in the *Gloucester*, next to the eastward of
us, threw himself upon the *Plutón* and the *Furor* with a vigor
and gallantry that excited our admiration. His danger was not
only from the enemy's guns, but from the *Indiana's* and the
Iowa's. In his official report he states that he was reassured as
to the risk he ran from our battle-ship's batteries by the signal
made by Captain Taylor, 'Gunboats close in.' The signal I

really made was, 'Enemy's torpedo-boats coming out,' and the
Gloucester did, in fact, narrowly escape being fired upon by
both the *Iowa* and the *Indiana*, the smoke of the battle con-
cealing her position from us, as it had obscured our signals a
few minutes before, and caused them to be misinterpreted by
the *Gloucester*. All's well that ends well. We did not fire at her."
Wainwright himself wrote:

"The Maxim one-pounders from the *Plutón* and the *Furor*
appeared likely to be our most dangerous enemies. When we
came within three thousand yards of the destroyers these guns
began to play rapidly in our direction. Their fire could be traced
by the splashes of the projectiles coming closer and closer to us.
When they began to fall about twenty yards from us, and the
water was stirred up as if a hail-storm was raging, the fire suddenly ceased. Had these guns secured our range, the execution
on board would have been terrible, and the *Gloucester* would
have been disabed, if not sunk.

"When within twelve hundred yards I ordered the two
small Colt rifles to open fire. . . . After the action our prisoners
spoke of the deadly effect of these guns."

It was probably the battleships that were too much for the
Spanish destroyers. "The rapid-fire batteries of the *Indiana*,
Iowa, and *Oregon* were turned on the venturesome little craft,"
wrote Captain Evans. "In a moment the water was boiling about
them, and before very long one was seen to be in distress. A
great column of steam fringed with coal and coal-dust arose
from her fifty to one hundred feet in the air, and we knew that
her boiler was done for. A large projectile, we believed from
the *Iowa*, seemed to cut her in two. At the same moment she
fired a shell which passed within six feet of my head; then she
swung slowly around under the tremendous fire of the *Gloucester*
and disappeared."

As the *Gloucester* closed in on the Spanish vessels, wrote
Wainwright, "I could see that the *Plutón* was slowing down, as

the distance lessened between her and the *Furor,* and it soon became apparent that she was disabled. . . . I now ordered the battery to be concentrated on the *[Furor].* We were within six hundred yards of her, and every shot appeared to strike. And now came the most exciting moment of the day: the *Plutón* was run on the rocks, and blew up; and at the same time the *Furor* turned toward us. It appeared to be a critical situation. She might succeed in torpedoing us, or she might escape up the harbor. But as she continued to circle, it became evident that she was disabled, and her helm was jammed over. Our fire had been too much for her."

12

A Fourth
of July Present

As the *Furor* turned toward us," wrote Lieutenant Commander Richard Wainwright of the *Gloucester,* "the flagship *New York,* coming up from the east under the fire of all the batteries, let drive two or three shots at her. I hoisted the signal, 'Enemy's vessels destroyed.' She gave us three cheers, and kept on under high speed after the big vessels."

Admiral Sampson and the *New York* arrived at about 10:15, just in time to see the end of the destroyers. Dressed in leggings and spurs, ready to ride to his rendezvous with General Shafter, he had been standing on the quarter-deck when he saw a puff of white smoke near the Morro: "I at once sent to the bridge the order: 'Put the helm aport and turn back immediately.' . . . Before the flagship had turned, a Spanish vessel appeared at the entrance, coming out under full steam. I sent at once for the chief engineer and directed him to light all the furnace fires, which he assured me had already been done. . . . The first thought was, 'Oh, that we had wings!'"

All that morning the *New York* chased after the combatants, exasperatingly within sight, but out of range, of the fleeing Spanish fleet, while Commodore Schley's *Brooklyn* was in the thick of the fight.

When the *Brooklyn* emerged from its turn and came out of the cloud of smoke, she seemed for a moment to be alone with the four Spanish cruisers. "I did not know then that the battle-ships could possibly keep up with their speed," Schley testified, "but I said to [Captain Cook]: 'We must stay with this crowd.' I had no idea we would escape."

A few minutes later, Schley "saw the *Oregon* breaking through the cloud-envelope. . . . I had hoisted the signals of 'Close up' and 'Follow the flag' . . . and I saw it repeated to our other ships." All the American ships were firing heavily at the Spaniards. "The *Brooklyn* and *Oregon* were a sheet of flame. I never saw such a fire; and never realized what rapid gun firing really meant before." Soon Schley saw that the *María Teresa* was badly damaged. "I said to Captain Cook . . . 'We have got one. Keep the boys below informed of all the movements. They can't see; and they want to know.'"

Aboard the *Oregon* Lieutenant Edward W. Eberle, in command of the forward turret, witnessed the destruction of the *María Teresa*:

"The *Teresa* was farther offshore than the other three vessels, and was being passed by them. We brought her sharp on our starboard bow, and as we gained on her our forward guns engaged her at two thousand yards' range, when (about ten minutes after ten) we discovered her to be on fire. The *Teresa* was soon left behind by the other vessels. Smoke and flames were pouring from her upper works, and the sight of her hope-less condition served to double the energy of our ships, for their fire became more rapid and deadly then ever. The *Oregon, Texas,* and *Iowa* hurled their terrific broadsides into her as she turned inshore and steamed slowly for the beach at Juan Gonzales, six miles from Santiago. Only forty minutes had elapsed since the stately *Teresa* had led the column out of the harbor. She boldly went to her death, fighting her guns until overwhelmed by fire and shell.

"The *Oregon* now charged on after the *Oquendo*, and opened on her with the forward guns, and also with all the guns of the starboard battery as soon as they could be brought to bear. . . . We closed rapidly . . . and, at a range of nine hundred yards, poured into her the hottest and most destructive fire of that eventful day. Each gun-captain fought his gun as if the victory depended upon him alone, and within twelve minutes after the *Teresa* had given up the fight the *Oquendo* was burning fiercely. She too turned inshore, with port helm heading slightly to the eastward; and as we drew her abeam, our guns raked her unmercifully. The *Oquendo* made the pluckiest fight and suffered the most severe punishment, as is attested by her torn and battered hull, which rested upon the beach half a mile west of the *Teresa*. When flames burst from the *Oquendo*, and she turned inshore, Captain Clark, who was standing on top of the forward thirteen-inch turret, called out to me, 'We have settled another; look out for the rest!' This was answered by a mighty cheer, which was repeated through the ammunition passages and magazines, and down among the heroes of the boiler- and engine-rooms.

"With bulldog determination, the *Oregon* continued on in her mad race after the *Vizcaya*, now two miles away, and opened with the forward guns. The *Brooklyn*, still on our port bow, was apparently about two miles off the *Vizcaya*'s port beam, and all three vessels were firing furiously. The *Colón*, now far ahead and close inshore, was increasing her lead."

Commodore Schley, standing beside the conning tower on the *Brooklyn*, feared that the Spanish vessels were gaining in the race. He sent Yeoman George Ellis to check the range of the

Vizcaya; at that moment a shell decapitated Ellis. Two officers lifted the body to throw it overboard, but Schley stopped them. "I thought that one who had fallen so gallantly deserved to be buried like a Christian." He was the only American killed during the engagement.

The *Brooklyn* and *Oregon,* followed by the *Texas,* closed in on the *Vizcaya.* Lieutenant Eberle of the *Oregon* wrote:

"Our speed steadily increased, and when we were about three thousand yards from the *Vizcaya,* [she] swung offshore and headed across our bow, firing her forward guns at the *Brooklyn* and her port ones at us. By this manoeuver the *Vizcaya* exposed her broadside to us, and a big shell from one of our turret guns seemed to strike her in the port bow, [and] she immediately resumed her former course. A few minutes later, at about a quarter to eleven, the man in the fighting-top reported that a thirteen-inch shell had struck her amidships, heeling her to starboard and sending up a volume of steam and smoke. Cheer after cheer rang through the ship, and our gun fire increased in rapidity. The *Vizcaya* was on fire and heading for the shore! Captain Clark, who had been moving about the decks commending officers and men for their good work, and telling his 'children' not to expose themselves needlessly, was at this instant standing on top of the after thirteen-inch turret, conversing with the officer of that turret. The turret-officer was deploring the fact that his guns would not bear on the enemy's remaining ships, when suddenly the burning *Vizcaya* was seen off our starboard bow, heading for the beach, and the captain exclaimed, 'There's your chance! There's your chance!' and in another moment the after-turret was thundering away with awful effect. The close range enabled our six-pounders to play havoc with the *Vizcaya's* upper works, and our fire was very heavy until she drew abaft our starboard beam, when, at eleven o'clock, she hauled down her colors and ran ashore at Aserraderos, eighteen miles from the Morro. This made the third large burning wreck within ninety minutes.

"When the *Vizcaya* gave up the fight and headed for the shore, the *Brooklyn* hoisted the signal, 'Well done, *Oregon*'; and then began the grandest chase in naval history. The *Colón* was now six miles ahead, and for a time it looked as if she might escape; but our efficient engineer department proved equal to the occasion, and our speed increased to more than sixteen knots. The *Brooklyn*, now broad off our port bow, was steering for the distant headland to cut off the *Colón*, while we were steadily edging in on her and forcing her nearer the shore.

"We sent our men to dinner by watches; but after getting a bite, they returned to deck to follow the exciting chase and take a pull at their pipes." Because of the slight damage to the American ships, the whole fight seemed to officers and men alike more a magnificent sporting spectacle than a grim and bloody battle. Captain Evans later wrote:

"I discovered a cadet, lately from Annapolis, standing on the forward turret of the *Iowa*, deliberately tilting a camera in his efforts to get a snap shot at the *Oquendo* while the machine-guns of that ship were making the air sing. I think he got his snap shot, and he will probably remember for many years to come the few words I addressed to him." Aboard the *Oregon*, during the chase after the *Colón*, Cadet C. R. Miller roamed the deck, taking snapshots of the officers and crew in holiday spirit.

Some distance behind, Admiral Sampson, still wearing his spurs, was witness to the chase as the *New York* gradually steamed within sight of the pursuers. W. A. M. Goode reported:

"The decks of the flagship trembled with the screw's vibrations. The *Colón* was supposed to have a speed of twenty knots. We knew the *Oregon* and the *Texas* and the *Vixen* could not make that, and we doubted if the *Brooklyn* could, with her foul bottom. We were making our level best, and it was more than we had dared to hope after our long wait in the warm waters of the South. Knot after knot we covered, and the outlines of the *Colón* grew plainer. At first we thought this was imagination; it seemed impossible. But there was no mistake; we were surely gaining, both on our own ships and upon the enemy. Soon after noon we could clearly make out the positions of the pursuing ships. The *Colón* was well inland, as close as we were to the shore, and dead ahead of us. On our port bow were the *Vixen* and the *Texas*. Well head of them was the *Oregon*, apparently keeping pace with the *Colón*, and at this we marvelled, for the *Oregon* is a battle-ship with a maximum speed of sixteen knots, and she had travelled many miles since she last saw dry-dock. Away outside the *Oregon*, whether ahead or abeam we could not tell, was the *Brooklyn*."

"The *Oregon* kept a parallel course about three hundred yards inside ours," wrote Captain Cook of the *Brooklyn*. "The *Colón* kept close to the land, running into all the bights. We steadily gained on her and were getting more steam all the time. We had four main and one auxiliary boiler on, and the remaining one and the other auxiliary were nearly ready."

As the chase continued, recalled Lieutenant Eberle:

"The *Brooklyn* signalled, 'She seems built in Italy'; and Captain Clark told the signal-officer to answer with the following message: 'She may have been built in Italy, but she will end on the coast of Cuba.'

"As we dashed onward, slowly gaining, and soon to be within range, the enthusiasm was at high pitch. An old boatswain's mate stationed in the fighting-top gave way to his excited feelings, and yelled through a megaphone, 'Oh, captain, I say, can't you give her a thirteen-inch shell, for God's sake!' The men in the engineer force, ever unmindful of the frightful heat, were straining every muscle to its utmost, and their heroic officers were assisting the exhausted firemen to feed the roaring furnaces."

Seaman R. Cross wrote in his diary: "The poor men in the fire-room was working like horses, and to cheer them up we passed the word down the ventlators how things was going on, and they passed the word back if we would cut them down they would get us to where we could do it. So we . . . settled down for a good chase for the *Colón*. I thought she was going to run away from us. But she had to make a curv and we headed for a point that she had to come out at."

Lieutenant Eberle explained:

"Several times the *Colón* turned in as if looking for a good place to run ashore, but each time changed her mind and continued to run for her life. It was ten minutes to one when Captain Clark gave me orders to 'try a thirteen-inch shell on her'; and soon an 1100-pound projectile was flying after her. The chief engineer was just coming on deck to ask the captain to fire a gun in order to encourage his exhausted men; and when they heard the old thirteen-inch roar, they knew that we were within range, and made the effort of their lives.

"The scene on the *Oregon*'s decks at this time was most inspiring. Officers and men were crowded on top of the forward turrets, and some were aloft, all eager to see the final work of that great day. The *Brooklyn* fired a few eight-inch shells, and we fired two eight-inch; but all fell short, and the eight-inch guns ceased firing. The *Colón* also fired a few shots, but they all fell far short of their mark. Our forward thirteen-inch guns continued to fire slowly and deliberately, with increasing range, and the sixth shot, at a range of ninety-five hundred yards (nearly five miles), dropped just ahead of the *Colón*, whereupon she headed for the shore. Our men were cheering wildly, and a few minutes later, at twelve minutes after one o'clock, a thirteen-inch shell struck under the *Colón*'s stern. Immediately her colors dropped in a heap at the foot of the flagstaff. The bugle sounded 'Cease firing!' The *Colón* had surrendered, and the last shot of July 3 had been fired.

"That was a moment to live for. Suddenly the thunder of heavy guns was replaced by the strains of 'The Star Spangled Banner' from the band. On our forward deck, five hundred and fifty men, mostly bare to the waist, and begrimed with powder, smoke, and coal-dust, were embracing one another, and cheering. . . .

"At the time of the *Colón's* surrender the *Brooklyn* was off our port bow, while between six and seven miles astern, and hull down, we saw the masts of two vessels which . . . proved to be the *New York* and *Texas*. These two vessels and the *Vixen* joined us at about twenty minutes after two, just as the *Brooklyn's* boat was returning from the *Colón*."

The fight was scarcely over when the great dispute began whether Commodore Schley or Admiral Sampson should receive credit for the victory. George Graham, a newspaperman aboard the *Brooklyn*, wrote:

"Commodore Schley ordered the signal raised: 'A glorious victory has been achieved. Details later.' . . . Vainly the signal officers on the bridge watched the *New York* for even the courtesy of an answering pennant showing that she understood our signal.

"Nevertheless, as the *New York* approached rapidly, Commodore Schley ordered another signal set, 'This is a great day for our country.' Instead of an answering pennant to this signal, there went up on the signal halyards of the *New York* a set of flags, which at first officers and men alike on the *Brooklyn* hoped to be a message of congratulation, but which proved to be a terse command, 'Report your casualties.'

"'Report your casualties,' repeated Schley, turning on his heel and walking over to the other side of the bridge, a pained expression on his face; and up to our signal masts went the flags, 'One dead and two wounded.'"

After four o'clock, Admiral Sampson ordered the *Oregon* to take charge of the prize. Lieutenant Eberle wrote, "When our prize crew reached the *Colón*, they found fifteen feet of water in her engine-rooms, and all valves open. The prisoners were immediately sent aft on the quarter-deck, and, with their effects, were transferred to the *Resolute*."

"The condition of the crew of the *Colón* was anything but satisfactory," asserted another officer. "Her firemen and coal-passers had been on shore in the trenches without food for thirty-six hours, and by some mistake there was no food prepared for them when they were embarked. To make up for this, they were liberally dosed with brandy to brace them up, and the result was not bad for the first hour; but then the reaction came. . . . One of the first duties of the prize crew was to break or throw overboard the half-emptied brandy bottles lying about the decks."

"While they were being transferred, our officers and men worked like beavers to keep the *Colón* afloat," Eberle remembered; "but their efforts were in vain, for at eleven o'clock that night she listed to starboard and turned over on her side, our officers leaving her just as she went over. . . . The next morning we started to our station at Santiago. The burning and battered wrecks strewn along the beach made a pitiful picture. Floating about them were uniforms, boxes, trunks, and here and there bodies of the dead."

The scenes of carnage created in the exhausted officers and men an attitude of compassion toward the vanquished and relief over escaping miraculously without heavy casualties, as much as exultation over the victory. The pious Captain Philip was reported as warning, "Don't cheer, men; those poor devils are dying." His chaplain later protested that Philip must have said "fellows" and not "devils." Certain it is that Captain Philip, shortly after the battle, according to T. M. Dieuaide, a correspondent on the *Texas*, called all hands aft. "The five hundred men of the ship trooped to the quarter-deck, which was still snow-white with the saltpeter from the guns, and listened reverently while Captain Philip offered thanks to God for their preservation from the perils of battle."

Through the hectic afternoon and into the evening of July 3, the American ships hurried about their rescue work, picking up men from the water, from the beaches (where the Spaniards feared the hostility of the Cubans), and from the burning ships. Lieutenant Thomas C. Wood of the *Gloucester* reported:

"I was ordered to save what life I could from the *Oquendo*, hard and fast ashore, and burning furiously. . . . On going alongside, as near as practicable owing to the surf and great heat from the burning vessel, I could see none of her officers and crew, except some twenty or thirty crowded on the forecastle and hanging by ropes from her bows; and these I succeeded in rescuing and putting aboard our ship, together with some ten or twelve whom I found floating on fragments of wreck. The burning cruiser, her plates many of them burst outward and red-hot, the roar of the flames, the constant explosions of small-arm ammunition from her guns or her boilers—this with the cries of the wretches on her bows for help, all made a scene which was indescribably impressive."

The *Iowa* came to the rescue of the officers and men who had jumped overboard from the *Vizcaya*. Captain Evans recalled:

"The ship had grounded about four hundred yards from the beach, and between her and the shore was a sand-spit on which many had taken refuge, the water being about up to their armpits. The Cuban insurgents had opened fire on them from the shore, and with a glass I could see plainly the bullets snipping the water up among them. The sharks, made ravenous by the blood of the wounded, were attacking them from the outside. Many of the wounded still remained on the deck of the *Vizcaya*, crowded on the forward and after ends of her, and were likely to be burned to death by the rapidly heating ship. . . .

"The torpedo-boat *Ericsson* and the auxiliary *Hist* came along about this time, and were sent in to assist in getting off the prisoners. Our boats soon began to arrive, filled with horribly mangled men. The effect of our shell fire had been most terrific, as was shown by wounds of these unfortunates."

When Captain Evans learned that Captain Don Antonio Eulate, commander of the *Vizcaya*, was coming aboard, he acted

New York *signaling at the close of the battle*

Wreck of Vizcaya

with that courtesy toward a fellow officer and gentleman with which the American officers treated their Spanish counterparts. Many of them had known each other for years, meeting in foreign ports and at naval reviews:

"As the boat approached the gangway I saw that Captain Eulate was wounded, and a chair was slung and lowered for his accommodation. . . . There was a foot of water in [the bottom of the boat], and in this rolled two dead men, terribly torn to pieces by fragments of shells; the water was red with their blood. In the stern-sheets sat Captain Eulate, supported by one of our naval cadets. . . . As the unfortunate captain was raised over the side, and the chair on which he sat placed on the quarter-deck, the guard presented arms, the officer of the deck saluted, and the Spanish prisoners already on board stood at attention. Captain Eulate slowly straightened himself up, with an effort unbuckled his sword-belt, kissed the hilt of his sword, and with a graceful bow presented it to me. I declined the sword. . . .

"Taking the captain's arm, I conducted him aft on our way to the cabin, where the medical officers were waiting to dress his wounds. . . . As we reached the head of the cabin ladder, he turned toward his ship, and, stretching up his right hand, exclaimed, 'Adios *Vizcaya!*' As the words left his lips, the forward magazine of the *Vizcaya* exploded with a tremendous roar, and a column of smoke went up that was seen fifteen miles away."

The Americans treated Admiral Cervera almost with awe when they captured him. He had succeeded in swimming ashore, and was pulled through the surf on a lifeline to one of the *Gloucester's* boats. "When I saw that gallant gentleman in his wringing wet underclothes, I felt as if I were a culprit," wrote Wainwright. At lunch, Lieutenant Harry. P. Huse ate with Cervera and some of his officers:

"Far from being depressed, the admiral was in high spirits. He had done his duty to the utmost limits, and was relieved of the terrible burden of responsibility that had weighed upon him since leaving the Cape Verde Islands. Perhaps, also, he wished to cheer his fellow-prisoners, for he gave full rein to his naturally genial temperament. I referred to the meagerness of our fare. The admiral expressed his satisfaction at having a meal before him, as he had had only a cup of chocolate brought to him on deck by his servant, very early in the morning, before starting out. For a moment there was silence, and perhaps the same thought occurred to all of us: what great changes have taken place since breakfast!"

The heavier weight of the American naval armament had created serious odds against the Spanish fleet. As Captain Chadwick later pointed out in his history of the war: "Some Spanish guns and ammunition were defective and the latter scant; there had been no target practice. . . . There were six heavy ships against four; fourteen 12- and 13-inch guns against six 11-inch; thirty 8-inch against none on the Spanish side of that calibre; forty-four 6-inch, 5-inch, and 4-inch against thirty-six 5.5- and 4.7-inch; ninety-six 6-pounders against thirty-eight Spanish."

The Americans lost one killed, and one seriously wounded; the Spanish sustained 323 killed and 151 wounded out of 2,227 men, according to Captain Concas. The Americans took 1,813 prisoners; a handful of others made their way into the Spanish lines at Santiago.

Despite the overwhelming nature of the victory, there were discomforting aspects to it. The slow American vessels had overhauled several of the Spanish vessels only because of their foul bottoms. Badly armored American vessels and unprotected crews had been saved from sinking and slaughter only by the incredibly defective Spanish marksmanship, and truly phenomenal good fortune. Conversely, while the American fire was heavy, it seemed to be effective mainly because it started blazes on the flooring and woodwork of the Spanish ships. A sailor from the *Oquendo* told Captain Chadwick the next day, "The ship was a slaughter pen." Captain Concas declared that on the bridge of the *María Teresa*, "all who were outside the conning-tower were killed and wounded, and I personally saw seven projectiles strike there, one of which, no doubt of large calibre, cut one of my orderlies in two, and another put me and my whole staff out of action." Nevertheless, the board of officers who examined the four destroyed Spanish ships found evidence of only 122 visible hits. The Americans had fired 9,433 shots. Even if the number of hits was double what the board found, the record was not impressive.

These misgivings came later and helped spur further modernization of the navy in the early 1900's.

On the afternoon of July 3, 1898, there was no discordant note to sully the victory—except the dispute over the credit for it, already emerging among the proponents of Sampson and Schley. By the time it was carried to a naval court of inquiry in 1903, it seemed almost to overshadow the battle. On the evening of July 3, one of Admiral Sampson's officers reached the cable office at Siboney, managed to prevent the sending of Schley's dispatch, and sent Sampson's announcement:

"The fleet under my command offers the nation, as a Fourth of July present, the whole of Cervera's fleet."

In Washington, Secretary of War Alger, worried over Shafter's warning that he might withdraw from San Juan heights, received the news of the naval victory with relief:

"At two o'clock on the morning of July 4th I walked home, with the newsboys crying in my ears the joyful tidings of 'Full account of the destruction of the Spanish fleet!' I also had with me the last massage from General Shafter, received at a quarter past one. It contained but a single sentence—

"'I SHALL HOLD MY PRESENT POSITION.'"

Hoisting the flag in Santiago, by Clinedinst

13

Siege of Santiago

The height of ironies in this ironic war was that in the days after the destruction of the Spanish fleet, the American troops had to risk new disaster in order to capture a city that was no longer of serious military importance. They must storm the barbed-wire entanglement and strong fortifications of Santiago at a cost sure to be heavier than the sixteen hundred casualties they had already sustained. Or they must wait in the steaming, muddy trenches, with each day's shower heavier, hoping that starvation would conquer the Spaniards before disease could immobilize the American army. One way or another, the Americans must capture Santiago and its empty harbor in order to justify their earlier expenditure in men and to guard their military prestige. Little could be gained; much was to be risked.

General Shafter was no butcher. Rather than again cast the iron dice of assault, he gambled that he could win Santiago by siege before yellow fever struck. On the evening of July 3, he cabled Washington: "From news just received of escape of fleet am satisfied place will be surrendered."

The War Department was ready to aid Shafter in his gamble by rushing him additional troops and artillery. Already in reply to his pleas it had wired: "You can have whatever re-enforcement you want. Wire what additional troops you desire and they will be sent as rapidly as transports can be secured. In addition to the 2,700 troops now en route from Tampa, the *St. Paul* and *Duchess* will leave Newport News not later than Wednesday with 3,000 troops of Garretson's brigade; the *St. Louis, Yale,* and *Columbia* will sail probably from Charleston, carrying 4,000 more, and others will be sent from Tampa as you may request."

Day by day, Shafter's lines extended further around Santiago and his trenches became more formidable; more and more guns pointed from their implacements down into the city. Outside Morro Castle, the naval vessels, which adamantly refused to risk running the channel into Santiago, did still ride, their guns ready to bombard the Spaniards.

From this strong position, General Shafter with considerable skill undertook long and tedious negotiations with the Spanish commander. General Linares had been wounded in the shoulder; General José Toral was in command. Like other of the Spanish officers, he compensated with bravery for any deficiencies in skill. He might be led to capitulate rather than fight futilely, but only if he could do so with his honor unimpaired. Nor would he surrender without permission from his superiors.

Shafter, on the morning of July 3, before he knew of Cervera's sortie, had sent his first ultimatum to Toral: he must surrender or suffer bombardment—he should inform foreigners and women and children to leave the city before ten o'clock of July 4. In the afternoon, after the Spanish fleet had left, Toral replied: "This city will not surrender. . . . I will inform the foreign consuls and inhabitants of . . . your message."

McClernand pointed out that Shafter, despite Toral's rebuff, had achieved one of his aims, "to secure a truce that would give our tired Army some hours rest." Shafter ordered the troops to cease firing, and General Wheeler at ten in the morning sent Colonel J. H. Dorst under a flag of truce to deliver the ultimatum to the Spanish forces.

The truce was a welcome surcease. "Everybody drew a long breath and thanked God," asserted Lieutenant Pershing. "It was possible once more to walk erect; however, the echoes of the last three days were slow to die away and at the breaking of a bough or the rustling of a leaf, there was a temptation to duck. Officers and soldiers of both armies were glad, and stood in the lines facing each other with a curiosity mingled with respect."

"I went up to the top of the trenches and I could see the town's people moving about and the soldiers cooking their dinners," Frank Knox wrote home. "Santiago is a pretty place. It seems a pity to lay it in ruins."

It was a nervous day, Lieutenant Orrin R. Wolfe of the Twenty-second Infantry remembered, because they did not yet know how Cervera's fleet had fared.

"We heard a terrific bombardment, although we were miles away. We could see splashes in the waters of Santiago Bay where shells from our Navy were apparently going over the hills and dropping. . . . We learned it was a Navy fight, and the first report we got was the Spanish Navy had sunk our ships and were headed towards Santiago to destroy our transports and supplies. It was a gloomy crowd for a while and we thought we would starve to death and die like rats. However, a little later in the afternoon . . . a member of General Shafter's staff rode along and gave us the correct dope of the fight, that our Navy had sunk most of the Spanish fleet and was pursuing what was left along the coast."

"The good news has inspired everybody," Shafter reported to the War Department. "A regimental band that had managed to keep its instruments on the line played 'The Star Spangled Banner' and 'There'll Be a Hot Time in the Old Town To-night,' men cheering from one end of the line to the other. Officers and men without even shelter tents have been soaking for five days in the afternoon rains, but all are happy."

A soggy but cheerful army celebrated the Fourth of July the next day. "At noon . . . the regiments were formed into line," declared Pershing, "and I had the pleasure of reading to my regiment a telegram from the President, extending the thanks and congratulations of the American people." In the afternoon, at the order of General Shafter, the regimental bands played in the front lines. This may have been the occasion when a correspondent heard the strains of "Fair Harvard" along part of the Rough Rider lines.

Underneath the gaiety was exhaustion, and beneath that disease. "It was only now," Stephen Bonsal wrote, "now that the strain was somewhat relieved, that we began to recognize that the men who had . . . shown such whipcord endurance, were but human after all. When they stumbled out of the noisome trenches . . . we saw that their faces were yellow, their eyes drawn, their cheeks hollow and sunken, their skin dry and crackling like parchment. . . . Men were found now in advanced stages of paludic, malarial, and even yellow fever who, while the fight was on and their good rifles were so needed on the firing-line, had not had the time or the heart to find out what ailed them."

Consequently, it was as much concern for his men as concern for the noncombatants in Santiago which led Shafter to agree to a postponement of the bombardment and a continuation of the truce. Ramsden, the British consul, went with other consuls into the American lines on July 3 to ask for more time. "We explained to them what a frightful act they were about to commit, and that, while doing no harm whatever to the Spanish Army, they would drive out to a barren country and starvation some 20,000 women and children and destroy their homes. The villages of Caney and Cuavitas and Dos Bocas were designated as places to which the people might go . . . but of course there was no food at either, and little shelter, and the country round was barren."

Shafter granted a delay to noon of July 5, and forwarded the consul's pleas to Washington. He did not see how he could possibly feed many refugees at El Caney, nor shelter many in houses still full of wounded. Near midnight, on the fourth, the navy bombarded the harbor entrance where the searchlights of the *Massachusetts* had made out a vessel apparently trying to escape. It was the *Reina Mercedes*, a rusting old three-thousand-ton cruiser, the guns of which were being used in shore defense. General Toral was trying to block the channel, since the Spanish fleet was gone and the underwater mines inadequate. Like the *Merrimac*, it sank at the wrong point. (After the war, the *Reina Mercedes* was raised and used as a barracks or receiving ship at Newport and later Annapolis.)

The populace of Santiago, hearing the bombardment, and thinking the fleet was forcing its way in, began pouring out. Pershing described the exodus:

"All day along the hot, dusty road leading from Santiago to El Caney, passed the long, white line; frail, hungry women carried a bundle of clothing, a parcel of food or an infant, while weak and helpless children trailed wearily at the skirts of their wretched mothers. An old man tottered along on his cane and behind him a puny lad helped an aged woman; old and young, women, children and decrepit men of every class—those refined and used to luxury, together with the ragged beggar— crowded each other in this narrow column. It was a pitiful sight; from daylight until dark the miserable procession trooped past. The suffering of the innocent is not the least of the horrors of war."

Stephen Crane rode to El Caney past the lines of refugees. "The vivid thing was the fact that these people did not visibly suffer," he wrote. "Somehow they were numb. There was not a tear. . . . But the town was now a vast parrot-cage of chattering refugees. . . .

"Pushing through the throng in the plaza we came in sight of the door of the church, and here was a strange scene. The church had been turned into a hospital for Spanish wounded who had fallen into American hands. . . . Framed then in the black archway was the altar table with the figure of a man upon it. He was naked save for a breech-clout and so close, so clear was the ecclesiastic suggestion, that one's mind leaped to a phantasy that this thin, pale figure had just been torn down from a cross. The flash of the impression was like light, and for this instant it illumined all the dark recesses of one's remotest idea of sacrilege, ghastly and wanton. . . .

"'Poor devil, I wonder if he'll pull through,' said [Sir Bryan] Leighton. An American surgeon and his assistants were intent over the prone figure. They wore white aprons. Something small and silvery flashed in the surgeon's hand. An assistant held the merciful sponge close to the man's nostrils, but he was writhing and moaning in some horrible dream of this artificial sleep. . . .

"'Good morning,' said the surgeon. He changed his knife to his left hand and gave me a wet palm. The tips of his fingers were wrinkled, shrunken, like those of a boy who had been in swimming too long."

Somehow the army and the Red Cross managed to provide the refugees with rudimentary medical care and some food. Kennan of the Red Cross stated: "To the refugees from Santiago at Caney—about fifteen thousand—we . . . forwarded, chiefly in army wagons furnished by General Shafter, six or eight tons of food, and were sending more as fast as we could land it in lighters through the surf."

The refugees were living miserably, but at least they were kept alive, and they were safe from bombardment. In theory, there was no reason why Shafter should not assault Santiago, but already he was trying through another expedient to lead General Toral toward surrender. Shafter asserted a few months later:

"Doctor Goodfellow . . . said that it would be a good thing to send the wounded prisoners into Santiago. I asked General Toral if he would take some dangerously wounded prisoners we had, into the town; that I could not give them proper care. He answered promptly that he would like to have them. Doctor Goodfellow went over the next morning and put them in ambulances, twenty-seven of them, and carried them into the town of Santiago with a military escort. It was something unheard of, and the men were received with the greatest joy. It was the first time the Spanish army had had opportunity of finding out what was going on outside, and I was told that the story those men gave of their treatment had a marked effect upon the men inside Santiago."

Shafter had also proposed that the Spanish exchange Lieutenant Hobson and the crew of the *Merrimac* for captured Spanish officers and men. The General in Chief of the Army of the Island of Cuba, General Blanco, agreed to this—and the armistice thus extended into the afternoon of July 6. The exchange took place after two o'clock. Crane wrote:

"Some of our Staff officers rode out with three Spanish officers—prisoners—these latter being blindfolded before they were taken through the American position. The army was majestically minding its own business in the long line of trenches when its eye caught sight of this little procession. 'What's that? What they goin' to do?' 'They're goin' to exchange Hobson.' Wherefore every man who was foot-free staked out a claim where he could get a good view of the liberated heroes, and two bands prepared to collaborate on 'The Star-Spangled Banner.' There was a very long wait through the sunshiny afternoon. . . .

"But suddenly the moment came. Along the cut roadway, toward the crowded soldiers, rode three men, and it could be seen that the central one wore the undress uniform of an officer of the United States navy. Most of the soldiers were sprawled out on the grass, bored and wearied in the sunshine. However, they aroused at the old circus-parade, torch-light procession cry, 'Here they come.' Then the men of the regular army did another thing. They arose *en masse* and came to 'Attention.' Then the men of the regular army did another thing. They slowly lifted every weather-beaten hat and drooped it until it touched the knee. Then there was a magnificent silence, broken only by the measured hoof-beats of the little company's horses as they rode through the gap. It was solemn, funereal, this splendid silent welcome of a brave man by men who stood on a hill which they had earned out of blood and death. . . .

"Then suddenly the whole scene went to rubbish. Before he reached the bottom of the hill, Hobson was bowing to right and left like another Boulanger. . . . However, one could thrill again when the tail of the procession appeared—an army waggon containing the blue-jackets of the *Merrimac* adventure. I remember grinning heads stuck out from under the canvas cover of the waggon. And the army spoke to the navy. 'Well, Jackie, how does it feel?' And the navy up and answered: 'Great! Much obliged to you fellers for comin' here.' 'Say, Jackie, what did they arrest ye for anyhow? Stealin' a dawg?' The navy still grinned. Here was no rubbish."

It was a critical point, for Shafter had instructed the American exchange commissioner, Lieutenant Miley, to notify the Spanish that hostilities would resume an hour after the exchange. Again he left a loophole, suggested to him by the navy. Shafter had tried in vain to persuade the navy to force an entrance into Santiago harbor; it did not want to risk losing ships. The War Department had even suggested running in a transport armored with bales of hay. Captain Chadwick, acting for Admiral Sampson, did work

Refugees waiting for food at El Caney church

Lieutenant Hobson coming down the road

Return of the crew of the Merrimac

out a plan of action with General Shafter, and drafted a new face-saving demand for surrender. It emphasized the hopelessness of the Spanish position and warned Toral that a joint army-navy bombardment of Santiago would begin at noon on July 9. This postponement was to give Toral time to refer the question to his home government. (Chadwick agreed with Shafter upon a twenty-four-hour bombardment to be followed by a marine assault upon the Socapa battery at the mouth of the harbor and a running of the harbor entrance by some smaller naval vessels.)

General Toral accepted the new armistice, cabled Madrid, and on July 8 made a counteroffer. He asserted that he had ample food and water for his troops; they were acclimated and less likely than the Americans to succumb to fever. Therefore the best he would propose was to relinquish the city of Santiago and the eastern half of the province of Santiago, provided he would be permitted to retreat from the area with his troops and matériel without being attacked. Under pressure from many of his officers, General Shafter recommended to Washington on July 9 that the offer be accepted. The War Department replied: "Your message recommending that Spanish troops be permitted to evacuate . . . is a great surprise and is not approved."

Shafter again demanded that Toral surrender unconditionally, setting a deadline of four o'clock on the afternoon of July 10. Toral declined and the truce came to an end.

The troops were delighted. Richard Harding Davis reported:

"The days . . . were filled with innumerable visits to the Spanish lines under flags of truce. To the men in the pits, who knew nothing of the exigencies of diplomacy, these virgin flags were as offensive as those of red are to the bull. The men had placed their own flags along the entire line of trenches; and though they afforded the enemy a perfect target and fixed our position as clearly as buoys mark out a race-course, the men wanted the flags there, and felt better at seeing them there, and so there they remained. The trenches formed a horseshoe curve five miles in length, and the entire line was defiantly decorated with our flags. . . .

"When [the men] saw crawling across the valley below the long white flag of truce, their watchfulness seemed wasted, their vigilance became a farce, and they mocked and scoffed at the white flag bitterly. These flags were sent in so frequently that the men compared them to the different war extras of a daily paper, and would ask, 'Has that ten o'clock edition gone in yet?' and, 'Is this the base-ball edition coming out now, or is it an extry?'"

Thus, the troops, well entrenched, welcomed the resumption of hostilities on July 10. Trooper J. O. Wells of the Rough Riders wrote in his diary:

"At four o'clock sharp the Spanish flag of truce went town, and it had scarcely fluttered to the ground when our dynamite guns opened, then the gatlings, rapid fire guns and mortars began to tear the air. The enemy responded weakly and contented themselves with cheering. At dusk the firing ceased, with a loss of but two men on our side. Our dynamite and rapid fire guns did splendid execution.

"MONDAY, JULY 11TH.

"At daybreak this morning our Artillery began hammering the Spanish entrenchments. I was relieved from the firing line about seven and returned just in time to see the First Illinois Infantry come up. They presented a fine sight, thirteen hundred strong, and all with bright new uniforms and clean flags. The Spaniards are more active to-day and we have suffered some loss from their shells. Our Artillery seems to fire in a half-hearted sort of way."

On the evening of July 10, the *Brooklyn* and *Indiana* fired eight-inch shells into Santiago for an hour. The next morning they resumed firing, joined by the flagship *New York*. Guided by signals from the shore, they vigorously bombarded the city from 9:35 until 12:45, when General Shafter requested them to cease. He had received instructions from Washington with which he wished to begin new surrender negotiations. The War Department had cabled him: "Should the Spaniards surrender unconditionally and wish to return to Spain they will be sent back at the expense of the United States government." With this lure, and with the warning that heavy reinforcements had arrived that morning, Shafter persuaded Toral again to communicate with his superiors and meanwhile suspend hostilities.

Several American transports had indeed arrived with reinforcements. Aboard the *Yale* was General Miles, top-ranking general in the army, who because of Shafter's illness had rushed to Cuba.

Shafter by this time was feeling fine, but impatient officers and men like Roosevelt were complaining of his "imcompetency and timidity." Roosevelt reported to Lodge on July 10: "We on the firing line are crazy just at present because Gen. Shafter is tacking and veering as to whether or not he will close with the Spaniards' request to allow them to walk out unmolested." This did not bother Shafter, who, joined by Miles, continued to tack and veer. He cheerfully told General Adelbert Ames that he was feeling well, although troubled with gout. Ames wrote his wife, July 11:

"I found Gen. Shafter sitting on a camp stool dressed in hickory shirt and a pair of blue trousers with a pair of dirty suspenders. . . . One foot was swathed in a dirty white cloth. His immense abdomen hung down, yes, actually hung down between his legs. . . . He was not a pleasing object either in figure or face."

General Miles found that the health of the troops was not as satisfactory as that of General Shafter. Three days earlier at Siboney, doctors had discovered what they thought to be three cases of yellow fever. General Miles, assuming that the buildings were infected, ordered them burned. This did nothing to stop the spread of the disease and, since it deprived many hospitalized soldiers of shelter, was a poor substitute for disinfection. Kennan added that the army had not even applied chloride of lime to the foul privies overflowing behind the houses:

"No attempt, apparently, had been made to clean or disinfect [the village]; no sanitary precautions had been taken or health regulations enforced; hundred of incredibly dirty and ragged Cubans . . . thronged the beach, evacuating their bowels in the bushes and throwing remnants of food about on the ground to rot in the hot sunshine; there was a dead and decomposing mule in one of the stagnant pools behind the village, and the whole place stank. If under such conditions, an epidemic of fever had not broken out, it would have been so strange as to border on the miraculous."

By the time General Miles arrived, there were over thirty cases of supposed yellow fever at Siboney alone. The troops besieging Santiago were falling ill at a similar rate. This was not surprising, since they were living under even more appalling conditions. Sanitation was impossible in the trenches and in their crude shelters on the slope of San Juan Hill; flies and mosquitoes plagued the men, and there was the stench from rotting mules and half-buried corpses that each day's rains washed back to the surface.

Amid the filth, the dearest desire of most soldiers was to bathe. "I do not at all mind other men's clothes being offensive to me," an officer told Richard Harding Davis, "but when I cannot go to sleep on account of my own it grows serious." Rough Rider Wells wrote on July 10:

"After being in the entrenchments last night, I got leave of absence and took a good swim. It is the first time I have had my clothes off in three weeks and I feel like a new man."

Unfortunately, the pool where most men went to bathe was the pond between San Juan Hill and Kettle Hill. Into it drained the water from the trenches and the camp on the slopes. In it also, soldiers claimed, were the remains of several Spaniards. The streams, muddied by the constant fording of troops and mule trains, were not much superior. From them came the drinking water, and although there was some effort to boil it, thirsty soldiers drank whatever water they could get.

Added to this, the soldiers day after day were drenched with rain. There had been heavy showers since they arrived. These served some useful purpose, since some men stripped and bathed in them. An occasional fastidious one, possessing soap, would lather in the shower, only to have it stop, leaving him gooey for another twenty-four hours.

On the night of July 11, it began to rain in earnest. Major Edward Vollrath of the Eighth Ohio, which had just landed that afternoon, reminisced: "Raging torrents of water swept around their feet while the downpour from above kept up incessantly. . . . Streaks of lightning would start ripping across the eastern heavens and rush like great trains of fire along the mountain tops, disappearing in the west. Then would come a stunning crack of thunder, until it seemed as if creation were tumbling into chaos. Sleep was an impossiblity as the camp was literally swamped. . . . That night is said to be known in the history of the Santiago campaign as 'the night it rained.'"

Even to the seasoned Roosevelt, it was a memorable night:

"By midnight my tent blew over. I had for the first time in a fortnight undressed myself completely, and I felt fully punished for my love of luxury when I jumped out into the driving downpour of tropic rain, and groped blindly in the darkness for my clothes as they lay in the liquid mud. . . . I . . . made my way to the kitchen tent where good Holderman, the Cherokee, wrapped me in dry blankets, and put me to sleep on a table."

The increasing storms created a further problem. They made unloading from the transports exceedingly dangerous and difficult, and transportation inland almost impossible. "The failure to establish any depot for provisions on the fighting-line, where there was hardly ever more than twenty-four hours' food ahead, made the risk very serious," Roosevelt later wrote. "If a hurricane had struck the transports, scattering them to the four winds, or if three days of heavy rain had completely broken up our communication, as they assuredly would have done, we would have been at starvation point on the front."

The Spanish command faced equally desperate conditons—although, of course, they tried to hide them from the besieging Americans. From his sickbed, General Linares cabled Madrid:

"Our troops are exhausted and sickly in an alarming proportion. Cannot be brought to the hospital—needing them in trenches. Cattle without fodder or hay. Fearful storm of rain, which has been pouring for past twenty-four hours. Soldiers without permanent shelter. Their only food rice, and not much of that. . . . Our losses were very heavy. . . . Unfortunately, the situation is desperate. The surrender is imminent, otherwise we will only gain time to prolong our agony. . . .

"The honor of arms has its limits, and I appeal to the judgment of the Government and of the entire Nation, whether these patient troops have not repeatedly saved it since May 18th—date of first bombardment."

Not knowing how eager the Spanish commanders were to surrender if they could obtain permission, General Miles on the evening of July 12 joined Shafter in urging Washington to accept Toral's withdrawal rather than surrender. The president and secretary of war remained adamant. Miles, if he had to attack, planned to land his fresh troops to the west of Santiago harbor, with the aid of the navy to enfilade the Spanish lines, and take them from the rear. Next he sent word through General Shafter to General Toral that the commanding general of the army had arrived and would like to meet him between the lines. This led to a conference between Toral and Miles and Shafter at noon July 13. Miles reported:

"I informed General Toral distinctly that I had left Washington six days before; that it was then the determination of the Government that this portion of the Spanish forces must either be destroyed or captured; that I was there with sufficient reinforcements to accomplish that object, and that if this was not the case any number of troops would be brought there as fast as steamers could bring them if it took 50,000 men. I told him that we offered him liberal terms, namely, to return his troops to Spain; and I also pointed out the fact that this was the only way in which his forces could return. . . .

"He said that under the Spanish law he was not permitted to surrender as long as he had ammunition and food, and that he must maintain the honor of the Spanish arms. My reply was that he had already accomplished that; that he must now surrender or take the consequences, and that I would give him until daylight the next morning to decide. He appealed for longer time, saying it was impossible for him to communicate with his superiors, and upon his request I granted him until 12 o'clock noon. . . .

"On meeting General Toral [on July 14] . . . he stated that he was prepared to surrender his command, and that such action was approved by Captain-General Blanco, who had authorized him to appoint commissioners to agree upon the clauses of capitulation . . . but that before final action it was proper that the Government at Madrid should know and approve of what was done. . . . I . . . stated that we would accept the surrender, under the condition that the Spanish troops should be repatriated by the United States."

General Toral asked General Shafter if this would include his entire command. Shafter later declared:

"Up to that time I knew nothing of his territorial command. And I said to him, 'What does your command consist of?' . . . He said, '11,500 men are here, 7,000 are at Guantánamo . . . 3,500 men at San Luis . . . and about 1,500 about twenty-five or thirty miles away.' I said, 'Certainly, it takes everything.' . . .

"I was simply thunderstruck that, of their own free will, they should give me 12,000 men that were absolutely beyond my reach."

Two irritating days of negotiations, misunderstanding, and delay followed. At one point Shafter cabled the War Department, "We may have to fight them yet." Finally the surrender ceremonies were set for July 17.

"Sunday, the 17th, came in with a bright and beautiful morning," General Wheeler recalled. Religious services were held on San Juan Hill. At the close of them, he declared, "I am pleased to say there will be no more fighting; the enemy has surrendered."

Wheeler later described the surrender ceremony:

"General Shafter, together with the generals and their staffs, rode to a large field in front of Santiago, accompanied by a troop of cavalry; there they met General Toral, who was also accompanied by a company of one hundred men. . . . General Shafter rode up to General Toral and presented him with the sword and spurs of the Spanish General Vara del Rey, who was killed at El Caney. The Spanish troops then presented arms, and the Spanish flag, which for three hundred eighty-two years had floated over the city, was pulled down and furled forever. The American officers and their cavalry troop also presented arms, after which the Spaniards filed to the left and returned to the city; where they, together with the entire Spanish army, were marched to the arsenal and their arms turned over to the American officials.

"The American generals then rode into town in column of twos, General Shafter and General Wheeler in front, and the other generals following in order of rank. . . . When we reached the palace we were met by all the officials, civil governor, archbishop, consuls, etc."

At noon, before thousands of spectators in the plaza, the officers lined up to witness the raising of the American flag over

The Sims-Dudley dynamite gun trained on Santiago

American and Spanish generals conferring

Services at which General Wheeler made announcement

Spanish troops marching through Santiago

Raising the American flag

the Governor's Palace. At this moment, an untoward incident almost marred the ceremony. Lieutenant C. D. Rhodes wrote in his diary:

"A war correspondent by the name of [Sylvester] Scovel, who represented the New York *World*, insisted in mounting to the roof of the governor's palace where the flag raising was to take place, but much to his indignation was ordered down by Colonel Miley, in charge of the ceremony. Thereupon Scovel appealed to General Shafter in a loud voice, while the general and his staff were standing before the assembled troops. . . . Some words followed, and I saw Scovel strike or attempt to strike General Shafter in the face. Scovel was hustled off by the soldiers and the ceremony proceeded." (It was not until the next day that Rhodes was sent to the ancient calaboose to release Scovel, who was to be expelled to Siboney. "Why, my boy," Scovel told him, "if you'll only send me to Siboney, I'll walk every step of the way! Never again do I want to pass a night in this hell-hole with all these creeping things!")

So it was, General Wheeler recorded, that as the cathedral clock struck twelve, the flag was hauled up the staff. "At the same moment twenty-one guns were fired and the band of the Sixth Cavalry struck up 'Hail Columbia!' The Ninth Infantry, which was drawn up in the plaza, presented arms to the American colors."

In a six-mile ring about Santiago, the American troops watched the flag go up. "All the regiments were lined along the pits," Rough Rider Allen McCurdy wrote his father, "and when the salute was fired, there was great cheering and enthusiasm."

General Wheeler, who through the campaign had again demonstrated his personal courage, found additional reason for rejoicing: "As we rode for the first time into Santiago we were struck by the excellent manner in which the Spanish lines were intrenched, and more especially by the formidable defences with which they had barricaded roads." The barbed-wire entanglement on the road resembled "nothing so much as a huge thick spider's-web with an enormous mass in the center. Behind this some ten or fifteen feet were barrels of an extraordinarily large size, filled with sand, stones, and concrete. . . . It would indeed, have been a hard task for American troops, were they ever so brave and courageous, to have taken a city by storm which was protected by such defences as these."

General Shafter's long and vacillating surrender negotiations had robbed him of his popularity among the troops and at home, but he had captured Santiago without another massive bloodletting—a hair's breadth ahead of the fever.

Troops cheering the surrender

14

Puerto Rican Campaign

The expedition to Puerto Rico, planned as one of the main campaigns of the war, turned out to be almost an anticlimax it proceeded so smoothly and relatively bloodlessly. After the surrender of Santiago, the war obviously could not last long. Indeed, the very next day, July 18, the Spanish ambassador in Paris asked the French to use their good offices to help arrange an armistice. That same day the War Department finally cabled to the impatient General Miles authorization to sail to Puerto Rico and, significantly, to hoist the United States flag.

General Miles had to act in the utmost haste. Fortunately he had kept his fresh troops on transports to prevent them from becoming fever-infected; additional men were to be rushed to him from the United States to meet on the Puerto Rican coast. He planned to land with the combined expeditions at Fajardo, and from there attack the nearby capital, San Juan. He reported:

"I started from Guantánamo on July 21 with 3,415 infantry and artillery, together with two companies of engineers and one company of the Signal Corps, on nine transports, convoyed by Captain Higginson's fleet, consisting of the battleship *Massachusetts* (flagship) and two smaller vessels. The *Yale* and *Columbia* were armed ships, but being loaded with troops, they were practically only available as transports. . . . Our effective force [was] about 3,300 men, and with that number we moved on the Island of Puerto Rico, at that time occupied by 8,233 Spanish regulars and 9,107 volunteers. . . .

"As all cablegrams concerning our landing place had passed over foreign cables, and as it was important to deceive the enemy (who, I afterwards learned, were marching to and intrenching the ground we were expected to occupy, at the very time we were taking possession of the southern coast of Puerto Rico), and nonarrival of launches, lighters, etc., the question of successfully disembarking the command became somewhat serious; and, after all hope of receiving any appliances of this kind had disappeared, I considered the advisability of finding a safe harbor and capturing necessary appliances from the enemy."

Consequently, General Miles changed his plans and decided to shift his landing to Guánica near Ponce, on the far end of the island from San Juan. Walter Millis has suggested also, in *The Martial Spirit,* that Miles did not want to share the credit for the conquest with the navy, which would have bombarded San Juan. Miles explained to Secretary Alger, "Marching across the country rather than under the guns of the fleet will have in every way a desirable effect on the inhabitants of this country." He seemed to ignore the fact that in the mountains he would have to traverse he was risking the repetition of several El Caneys.

For the soldiers and sailors on the transports off the coast of Cuba any risk seemed better than continued waiting. Also, they were only relatively fresh and healthy. Chief Yeoman James Taft Hatfield (on leave from his professorship at Northwestern

University) wrote in his diary July 16 of "the deadly monotony of *waiting*, the hardest, most wearing ordeal that can come. Heroism runs from the tips of one's fingers in this sultry air, lying in complete uncertainty off this fever-stricken coast." And on the twenty-second he noted, "Much typhoid fever on board. Filthy decks, no fresh water except at spigot. Angel of death with black wings seemed hovering inexorably over the ship."

The angel of death might have hovered even nearer as they approached the coast of Puerto Rico, since there was still one Spanish gunboat which might attack the unarmored vessel. No one especially worried. "It was like being set free from prison to leave the harbor of Guantánamo," Hatfield wrote for the Chicago *Record*. "We passed slowly along the northern coast of Haiti, running at night without lights so as to make our coming entirely unexpected, and on the early morning of July 25, a serene, beautiful day, we made directly for the port of Guánica, in the southwest corner of the island.

"Not knowing just what might be ahead, we went in fighting shape, the crews standing at their stations by their guns, which were trained, loaded and ready to fire. The saucy *Gloucester* ran ahead of us into the little harbor, flying an enormous American flag at her topmast, without stopping to inquire about batteries or torpedoes."

Lieutenant Harry P. Huse of the *Gloucester* reported:

"The force under my command, consisting of twenty-eight men and Lieutenant Wood, embarked in the cutter. We landed, without meeting with any opposition, at a little wharf, and the men were at once deployed to cover the beach. The Spanish flag was hauled down and our colors hoisted in their place.

"This drew the enemy's fire, who opened from the underbrush on the right flank. . . . The enemy's fire was well sustained but high, and no casualties resulted from it. At the northern limit of the village we built a wall across the highway and placed there the new Colt gun. . . . Meanwhile a boat . . . was

engaged in cutting out a large lighter, which came into immediate use in landing troops.

"About this time the *Gloucester* opened fire from her 3-
pounders and 6-pounders and the enemy retreated. A few minutes later the first contingent of the regular army, Colonel
Black's regiment of engineers, landed and rapidly pushed
beyond our lines."

"The bay is one of the best in the whole island, the banks to
the right being steep and forming a splendid wharf," Henry
Barrett Chamberlin reported in the Chicago *Record*. "Captain
Brown's engineers began the construction of a pier, and General
Miles himself, anxious to hasten the work, went about in his
steam launch, and, gathering together the pontoons dropped
from the transports, towed them to the point designated by the
engineers. The sight of the commander-in-chief doing orderly
service for the engineer officer was one of the sights which
added to the unusual in the Puerto Rico campaign."

The American forces at Guánica captured ten lighters, with
which they rapidly disembarked men and supplies. Within a few
hours, Richard Harding Davis reported, two thousand men of
the Sixth Illinois Volunteer Infantry and the Sixth Massachusetts were camped along the street. The inhabitants had
returned to their homes, and were selling their horses to the
officers. He wrote:

"The volunteers made themselves at home on the doorsteps
of the village, and dandled the naked yellow babies on their
knees. . . . The next morning there was an outpost skirmish, in
which the Sixth Massachusetts behaved well, and the next
evening there was a false alarm from the same regiment. This
called out the artillery and the Illinois regiments, and the picture made by the shining brown guns as they bumped through
the only street in the moonlight was sinister and impressive. To
those of us who had just come from Santiago the sight of the
women sitting on porches and rocking in bent-wood chairs, the

lighted swinging lamps with cut-glass pendants, and the pictures and mirrors on the walls which we saw that night through the open doors as we rode out to the pickets, seemed a part of some long-forgotten existence. . . .

"The alarm turned out to be a false one. . . . Later . . . our outposts on the hills would mistake stray mules and cattle for Spaniards, and kept up an unceasing fire about the camp until sunrise. Some of their bullets hit the transport on which General Miles was sleeping, and also the ship carrying the Red Cross nurses, who were delighted at being under fire, even though the fire came from the Sixth Illinois. From remarks made the next morning by General Miles, he did not seem to share in their delight."

Just what really happened is not entirely clear, since the action which Davis so humorously dismissed received serious attention from Chamberlin. "The next day," he reported, "came quite a brisk bit of skirmishing, in which the Massachusetts and Illinois regiments won their laurels by charging up a hill and putting to flight a squadron of cavalry, establishing themselves without loss, although the contest was one of smoky Springfields against smokeless repeating Mausers, with infantry on the aggressive, and the enemy's loss eight men killed and several wounded." General Miles reported:

"At daylight on the 26th of July . . . an attack was made upon a strong force of Spaniards near Yauco, and after a spirited and decisive engagement the enemy was defeated and driven back, giving us possession of the railroad and the highway to the city of Ponce.

"On the 27th of July Major-General [James Harrison] Wilson arrived [from the United States] . . . with General Ernst's brigade. The same day Commander Davis, of the *Dixie*, entered the port of Ponce [twenty miles to the east] and found that it was neither fortified nor mined. The next morning the fleet and transports, with General Wilson's command, moved

Spanish troops about to leave Mayaguez to fight the Americans

Battery B, Fourth Artillery, shelling blockhouse at Coamo, August 8, 1898

into the harbor of Port Ponce. The troops disembarked and marched to the city of Ponce, a distance of 2 miles, and we took formal possession of the city and adjacent country, the Spanish troops withdrawing on the military road to San Juan, and our troops being pushed well forward in that direction. In the meantime General Henry's command had been directed to proceed to Ponce, where he arrived shortly afterwards, joining General Wilson's command."

It was a gala occasion. Chamberlin of the Chicago *Record* reported:

"As the troopships steamed into the harbor hundreds of small boats filled with Puerto Ricans came out to extend a welcome. When the cutter in which the general rowed ashore started, the Puerto Ricans followed in seemingly endless procession, shouting, 'Viva Los Americanos,' while one hoarse-voiced individual . . . roared in broken English, 'Long live Washington.' . . .

"The entire population participated in the rejoicing. There was music in the streets and plazas; the houses were decorated with brilliant colors; the flags of a dozen nations flying over the consulates along the water front gave the place the appearance of a most energetic midway, while anything that bore the least likeness to the colors in the American flag was profusely used for decorating purposes. Streamers of red, white and blue flew from every balcony and every roof. The wharf, the streets, the roofs, the balconies were crowded with men, women and children in holiday attire. The firemen and the volunteers of the Puerto Rican army paraded in uniform and petitioned General Miles to be permitted to enlist in our army. . . . Hardly had the landing commenced than the commanding general and staff received invitations to dine with public officials, and the outlook for a social campaign of a month was more promising than the chances of blood-letting."

There had been little revolutionary sentiment in Puerto Rico, and only a few months earlier the Spanish had put into operation a new autonomous government. Nevertheless, the Puerto Ricans, expecting to fare better under a flag which had always stood for self-government rather than colonialism, were unbounded in their optimistic welcome. "The enthusiasm everywhere was intense," wrote Chamberlin, "and the sentiment of all was voiced by a prominent merchant, who declared in a speech that 'We are glad that the United States is to be our country.'"

The troops rejoiced not only over the welcome but even more because they were off the foul transports. Congressman Bertram T. Clayton, who served as captain of Troop C, New York Volunteer Cavalry, came down on the *Massachusetts*, carrying eleven hundred men and eleven hundred horses. "The ventilating fans were out of order," he wrote later, "it was a hot as the Sahara and the air between decks was putrid; to breathe it was like breathing sewer gas." As they approached the harbor at Ponce they ran onto a reef, where they were stuck for an additional day or so, while they watched others going ashore.

The Americans commandeered seventy lighters at Ponce. "I was very ably and cordially assisted by the Navy," reported General Miles, "which rendered invaluable aid in disembarking troops and supplies from the transports, using their steam launches to tow the lighters loaded with men and animals from the transports to the shore."

Finally the turn of the New York Volunteer Cavalry came. Irving Ruhland of Troop A wrote: "In the morning, after a breakfast of hardtack and coffee, we were towed ashore in a big lighter, and were in the enemy's country at last. . . . Natives came out to pole us alongside the big pier, and as we scrambled ashore pedlers of mangoes and greasy little corn cakes, and boys with boards piled high with 'dulce coca,' singing their melancholy song, plied us with their wares. We lingered on the pier for a while, and then marched to the square in front of the church, that was to be our camp until the horses were unloaded. The Philadelphians were already ensconced on the shady side of the church; some of them trying to get picket line posts to hold in the soggy ground. . . .

"Some of those who were not on guard or on the detail to unload horses and stores, slept on the narrow piazzas of the houses, or wherever a patch of shade could be found. Others wandered through the little town and brought back stories of endless cheap cigars and cheaper meals of rice and beans and an occasional egg. . . . We spent the night lying where we could— under shelter when it was to be found, for rain was certain to fall. Many, however, were content with the pebbly road. The scuttling of land crabs and attack of mosquitoes made the night far from happy.

"Milkmen appeared at dawn. . . . The milkmen milked the cows at the doorsteps directly into small-necked bottles. . . . Ox carts loaded with commissary stores soon filled the street—a slowly moving, patient procession. . . . Our horses began to come ashore as the day dragged along, and were picketed to the fence where the native washerwomen had been hanging their clothes." Unloading the horses was not too easy, as Leonard S. Horner of Troop A described it:

"This was done by swinging a derrick over to the side of the ship, having a rope attached to the end of the arm with a canvas sling on it, in which the horses and mules were tied, and then lowered to the scow. Doc Becker went down on the first scow and loaded it. It was a unique sensation, standing in the scow, the rise and fall of the heavy ground swell now dashing it against the side of the ship, now carrying it a few yards away; with what looked like an octopus coming down on you from thirty feet above, legs going every way. The man in the scow had the guide rope, and his first attempt, as the horse sprawled on the floor and scrambled for the side, was to grab the beast by the halter and jerk him back. It took good nerve."

Soon the troops were comfortably encamped near Ponce, at first in shelter tents along a barbed-wire fence. "The fence was soon hung from end to end with haversacks, canteens, blankets and underclothes of every size and color," wrote Ruhland; "ponchos and blankets were stretched from the tent-tops to the fence-posts to make larger the area protected from sun and rain."

General Miles established his forces ashore with deliberate slowness. Chamberlin of the Chicago *Record* wrote:

"During the first week of the occupation of Ponce the situation was one of curious interest. The forward movement was slow, not because the roads were other than magnificent boulevards, but rather because the commanding general was in no hurry. He was mapping out a plan of campaign almost perfect in its detail, for it was designed to win all that was sought with the minimum of blood-letting. . . .

"It was a jolly week . . . but it was not all play. Serious business was being conducted, and a lasting impression created. . . . The artillery arrived, and as the field pieces, drawn by large, strong American horses, rumbled through the narrow steets, the people looked on in awe, and then, as regiment after regiment of stalwart fellows from the west marched past in fighting trim, the conviction that the Americans were invincible took deeper root in the minds of the people, and the news spread inland and on to the coast beyond the second range of mountains, where the captain-general was marshaling his forces to resist the assault to come. . . .

"But one day, at a time when those not in the confidence of the commanding general had begun to look upon the campaign in Puerto Rico as a huge joke, word came to move, and with it definite, clean-cut information regarding what was to be done, how it was to be done, and what was to result when it had been done.

"Major-General [J. R.] Brooke, who had landed with his division of the army at Arroyo, forty miles to the east of Ponce, and had skirmished with the enemy while moving toward Guayama to the west of his base, was directed to push on to Cayey, thence to Aibonito. General Wilson was to take this command, with Ponce as a base, along the road leading through Juan Diaz and Coamo, and join with Brooke at Aibonito, and then this combined column was to proceed to Caguas, thence to Rio Piedras, taking the towns of Aguas Buenas and Guaynabo en route, and holding itself in readiness to move to San Juan from the southeast when word was given. General [Guy] Henry, with Ponce as a base, was to move to Adjutas, thence to Utuado, and continue north until Arecibo was reached. General [Theodore] Schwan, with Ponce as a base, was to take the road along the coast, operating through the country marked by Guayanilla, Yauco, San Germán, Mayagüez and Aguadilla, at the northwestern point of the island; from there he was to march east along the north coast, joining Henry at Arecibo, the two columns to continue to Dorado, thence to Bayamón, six miles from San Juan.

"This plan contemplated a movement practically covering all of Puerto Rico, and the dispositions of the columns were such as to make it possible to outflank the enemy at every point where he appeared in any considerable force. The idea of General Miles was to avoid loss of life wherever possible, and at the same time gradually push the Spaniards into San Juan, which . . . he intended to invest [and] capture."

"The generals lost no time in getting to work," reported Richard Harding Davis. "Juan Diaz was, in theatrical parlance, a one-night stand, and it surrendered without a fight to General Wilson, but the taking of Coamo, the next city on his list, was one of the prettiest skirmishes of the campaign." Davis chased after General Wilson on the morning of August 9:

"The while helmet of the general halted next to an open field of high yellow grass, where four brown guns pointed at a block-house on the hill above Coamo. As we drew up one of the guns roared and flashed, and a cloud of white smoke rushed forward and stopped as though it had struck a solid wall and then swept back again, hiding the gun and the men about it in a curtain of mist. The horses under the trees reared and tugged at their bridles and danced. . . . A few Mauser rifles answered the guns, but the bullets flew high and did no harm.

"The block-house smoked and crumbled and then burst into red flames. The artillery limbered up again and crawled off up a hill to the right, and Troop C, of Brooklyn, moved off still farther to the right and disappeared over a hill. All the infantry started forward. . . .

"On the other side of Coamo the Spaniards were hurrying across the bridge and out into the white road. On the hills above them the Sixteenth Regiment of Pennsylvania were waiting for them and opened fire. . . .

"The Spanish comandante seemed to wish to die. He galloped out of the road and into the meadow, where he was conspicuous from the top of his head to the hoofs of his horse. At one time he stood motionless . . . holding his reins easily and looking up at the firing line above. After he was killed the men in the trench along the road raised a while handkerchief on a stick and ceased firing."

This was the most serious battle of the Puerto Rican campaign. Six Americans were wounded, and the Spanish lost six men killed and thirty or forty wounded. Davis and several other correspondents, together with two members of General Wilson's staff, raced their horses down the road to see Coamo surrender. Davis wrote:

"The clatter [the horses] made in the empty streets was impressive. . . . They were excited by the shouts and by the flags, and they carried us, racing neck and neck, to the other end of Coamo. There we found, to our embarrassment, that it was empty of American troops, and that, unwittingly and unwillingly, we had been offered its surrender."

Several years later, Davis wrote that Stephen Crane, at the urging of his literary agent, had gone off by himself and single-handedly captured a town.

The advance in all directions went almost this easily. Davis reported: "General [Peter C.] Hains meanwhile had taken Guayama from four hundred Spaniards at the cost of one officer and four men wounded, all of the Fourth Ohio. On the 13th, General Schwan's regulars found the Spaniards intrenched in force at Las Marías and drove them back and out of Mayagüez, a city of 30,000 inhabitants. . . . General Stone engaged the enemy in a night skirmish beyond Adjuntas and drove the Spaniards back."

Several more attacks were about to begin on the morning of August 13 when word arrived than an armistice had been signed. Meanwhile the navy had captured Fajardo. Admiral Chadwick later pointed out that General Miles could have as easily landed there and marched forty level miles to San Juan rather than risk serious trouble in the mountain passes. But it made little difference, the Spanish forces in Puerto Rico were so defeatist.

General Miles gained relatively little glory from his exploits, not because of charges of defective strategy, but through Finley Peter Dunne's little gibe that it had been a moonlight picnic. Picnic it had been in many respects; most of the troops were able to embark on transports for home within thirty days after they had landed. But Richard Harding Davis challenged Dunne's insinuation:

"The reason the Spanish bull gored our men in Cuba and failed to touch them in Porto Rico was entirely due to the fact that Miles was an expert matador; so it was hardly fair to the commanding General and the gentlemen under him to send the Porto Rican campaign down into history as a picnic."

15

Expedition to
the Philippines

A jubilant public had thought when the first indirect reports of Admiral Dewey's triumph arrived that the United States had captured the entire Philippine archipelago. This was not so; the navy had done no more than seize the Spanish base at Cavite and blockade Manila. Had the United States gone no further, it might conceivably have later withdrawn, but even before Admiral Dewey's official report arrived in Washington, President McKinley came to a significant decision. He ordered American forces sent to the Philippines. This meant the occupation of at least Manila, which would almost certainly lead to American retention of a naval base, and probably to annexation of all the Philippines. Thus the United States would become a major power directly involved in the complicated international politics of the Far East.

General Miles on May 3 suggested sending various troop units; the following day President McKinely sent him written authorization and the assembly of troops and supplies at San Francisco began. It was many weeks before the first contingent could reach the Philippines. Admiral Dewey sent word from Cavite May 13:

"I am maintaining strict blockade of Manila by sea, and believe rebels are hemming in by land, although they are inactive. . . . I can take Manila at any moment. To retain possession and thus control Philippine Islands would require, in my best judgment, well-equipped force of 5,000 men. . . . One British, one French, two German, one Japanese men-of-war here observing."

Both the observing men-of-war and the insurgents in time created perplexing problems for Dewey. That of the insurgents developed rapidly after he allowed Emilio Aguinaldo, their exiled leader, to return and develop very considerable strength. He reported June 27:

"Aguinaldo, insurgent leader, with thirteen of his staff, arrived May 19, by permission, on *Nanshan*. Established self Cavite, outside arsenal, under the protection of our guns, and organized his army. I have had several conferences with him, generally of a personal nature. Consistently I have refrained from assisting him in any way with the force under my command, and on several occasions I have declined requests that I should do so, telling him the squadron could not act until the arrival of the United States troops. At the same time I have given him to understand that I consider insurgents as friends, being opposed to a common enemy. . . . I believe he expects to capture Manila without my assistance, but doubt ability, they not yet having many guns."

Aguinaldo had practically surrounded Manila and had occupied much of the area around Cavite, capturing twenty-five hundred Spanish prisoners. He assumed that the United

States would aid the Filipinos in winning their independence. On May 24, he proclaimed, "Now that the great and powerful North American nation have come to offer disinterested protection for the effort to secure the liberation of this country, I return to assume command of all the forces for the attainment of our lofty aspirations."

On July 1, Aguinaldo proclaimed himself president of the revolutionary Philippine republic, but already in Washington there was a disposition to feel that although the war was being fought to free Cuba, the Philippines would be legitimate spoils. Secretary of State W. R. Day sent word to the American consul in the Philippines:

"To obtain the unconditional personal assistance of General Aguinaldo . . . was proper, if in so doing he was not induced to form hopes which it might not be practicable to gratify. . . . The United States in entering upon the occupation of the islands as a result of its military operations in that quarter, will do so in the exercise of the rights which the state of war confers, and will expect from the inhabitants . . . that obedience which will be lawfully due from them."

This position could lead to an ominous future. Meanwhile, Admiral Dewey seemed to be suffering a more immediate menace from the German observing fleet of five ships, which was at least as strong as his force. It violated the blockade rules by moving freely about Manila Bay, communicating frequently with the Spanish, and menacing the insurgents. Dewey in later years enlarged these infractions in his mind until they assumed the proportions of a hostile plot. Rather, the Germans at worst were meddlesome onlookers, hopeful that the islands would become their spoils. On July 13, Admiral Dewey reported the most important incident of German interference:

"Aguinaldo informed me his troops had taken all of Subic Bay except Isla Grande, which they were prevented from taking by the German man-of-war *Irene*. On July 7 sent the *Raleigh* and

The Irene *and sister ships of German Asiatic Squadron*

General Merritt and staff aboard Newport

Signaling American advance to Navy and stringing wire, August 13, 1898

the *Concord* there; they took the island and about 1,300 men, with arms and ammunition; no resistance. The *Irene* retired from the bay on their arrival."

One other threat worried both Admiral Dewey and the American expedition crossing the Pacific during the early summer. This was the rumor of late May, confirmed in a Navy Department warning of June 18: "The Spanish fleet, two armored cruisers, six converted cruisers, four destroyers, reported off Ceuta, sailing to the east." Theoretically this last Spanish fleet under Admiral Manuel de la Camara was stronger than the United States Asiatic Squadron. What if it should defeat Dewey in Manila Bay and then ambush the American transports as they arrived in the Philippines? This eventuality was not likely, but Dewey laid careful plans for a possible Spanish attack. Troop commanders on the second group of transports, out of touch with the rest of the world for thirty days, could not help wondering if they would be met by Admiral Dewey or Admiral Camara.

The first group of three transports, carrying 117 officers and 2,382 men under Brigadier General Thomas M. Anderson, sailed from San Francisco May 25. From Honolulu eastward they were convoyed by the protected cruiser *Charleston*, which stopped en route to capture the Spanish island of Guam. According to rumor, modern fortifications and one or more gunboats defended the island. Captain Henry Glass consequently approached ready for a fight, and fired several shots at Fort Santa Cruz. There was no reply, for the guns had been taken elsewhere, and the Spanish authorities on the island did not even know war had been declared. The captain of the Port of San Luis exclaimed to Captain Glass:

"Why, Captain, we are without defenses at this port, as all of our forts have been dismantled. If it were only that you were entitled to a salute from us, we could not have fired it except from Agaña, as we have not even a field-piece on this bay."

General Anderson's troops arrived in Manila Bay on June 30, and began disembarking at Cavite the next day. They could do no more than hold the base there. After an interview with Aguinaldo, Anderson reported, "He did not seem pleased at the incoming of our land forces."

A larger contingent of troops, some thirty-five hundred men, sailed June 15 under Brigadier General Francis Vinton Greene. A third group of nearly five thousand officers and men under Brigadier General Arthur MacArthur (father of Douglas MacArthur) sailed June 27 and 28. Finally, the commanding general, Major General Wesley Merritt, and his staff embarked on June 29. A signal corps sergeant wrote home:

"What a magnificent send-off San Francisco gave us as we sailed out of the harbor that glorious 27th of June. The numberless steam whistles, the guns, flags flying everywhere, handkerchiefs waving. . . . Then the boys on the *Indiana* realized what the parting really meant, but we did not dwell long upon that, for as we passed [through the Golden Gate] a strong wind was blowing which steadily increased. After crossing the bar the sea was very rough, and I think nine hundred and ninety of the one thousand men on board were sea-sick.

"It was an exceedingly rough night—one might say a night of horror—you must know how crowded we were. . . . It was simply suffocating. A porthole leaked somewhere, and the water washed back and forth over our deck, carrying with it various articles which had been broken loose. I saw a large roast of beef, two boxes of hard-tack, two large coffee-pots, and some tin pans float past our room several times, making a most unearthly racket."

The next morning, the sergeant, lashed to a stanchion, had to wave signals to the other ships. "It was the wildest work I ever did," he wrote. "The seas were tremendous. Half a gale was blowing. We were in the trough of the sea, rolling so heavily it seemed as if every roll would be our last." But gradually the sea quieted, and the soldiers settled into the routine of the month-long voyage. One day the condenser of the *Newport* broke; while it was being repaired a private fished for sharks with a large piece of government beef, remarking, "The bait'll kill him with indigestion if I don't catch him with the hook."

Then came a delightful interlude in Honolulu. "The streets . . . were filled with the soldiers of our expedition," Frank Davis Millet reported, "most of them wearing the fragrant wreaths with which the hospitable islanders decorate themselves and their friends on festal occasions, and many with silk badges bearing the words 'Aloha nui to Our Boys in Blue.'"

The people of Honolulu were in a state of anticipatory excitement as they awaited word of annexation. Congress voted it the day the *Newport* arrived, July 6, but the news was a week reaching Hawaii. President Dole's private secretary wrote a friend:

"A salute of one hundred guns was fired from the Government battery. The Royal Hawaiian Band came down to the wharf and the crowd immediately formed into a procession, marching through the principal streets waving American flags. . . . I was in the middle of the crowd and 'yelled myself hoarse.' It is simply a great feeling to find that one is back in one's own country again."

Meanwhile the transports had continued their voyage, with the army commanders wondering if trouble with Admiral Camara lay ahead. They could not know that days before their arrival it had evaporated. After the victory at Santiago, the Navy Department had given orders to assemble a "flying squadron" to harass the coast of Spain. This had forced the Spanish government to recall Camara from Suez on July 8. Had he continued, his ships would have arrived so late and in such bad shape that they would have been no menace.

The really serious question facing General Merritt when he arrived in Manila was whether he could land his men and take

Manila relatively bloodlessly before the war ended. If he and Admiral Dewey acted deliberately and discreetly they need run little risk of serious fighting—with the Spaniards.

General Greene upon his arrival on July 17 found long, narrow peanut field lying just behind a sandy beach south of Manila, and decided to land his men there. "It was sufficiently large to accommodate seven or eight thousand men, and its northern edge was just out of range of musketry, but well within the range of field artillery in the Spanish lines," Greene reported. This seemed no serious obstacle, as the Spanish troops fired only in a desultory fashion, and feared the threat of serious retaliatory bombardment by Admiral Dewey's squadron. Greene's (and later MacArthur's) men landed in "cascos or native lighters, somewhat resembling the Chinese junk but without sails. Each of these was capable of carrying about two hundred men with their shelter tents, packs, and ten days' rations."

Thus Camp Dewey came into existence. The troops dug entrenchments and spent long, impatient hours crouched behind them, safe from the wildly fired Spanish bullets, but bored. They did not relish their rather unheroic role as a besieging force, and were not aware of Dewey's careful pressure for Spanish surrender. On the night of July 31–August 1, the men of the Tenth Pennsylvania answered the heavy but harmless Spanish fire, and in so doing gave it direction. In a two-hour interchange, the Americans lost ten killed and forty-three wounded. Night after night, the Spanish similarly opened fire, but Dewey restrained the American attackers. He explained to General Greene that it was better "to have small losses, night by night, in the trenches, than to run the risk of greater losses by premature attack."

But he added that the decision rested with Greene; he would bombard the Spanish if Greene gave the signal.

On August 7, Dewey gave the new Spanish governor-general, Fermin Jaudenes, forty-eight hours' notice prior to bombarding

Manila. This ended all firing until August 13, and initiated negotiations rather similar to those at Santiago. The governor-general would not surrender the city, but after several days let it be known through the Belgian consul that he would not offer serious resistance. Obviously he did not want to suffer the opprobrium at home of surrendering without fighting; neither did he want Manila to fall to the insurgents.

Admiral Dewey and General Merritt undertook, on August 13, the fighting of one of the most unusual battles in military and naval history. They planned it to be bloodless. "It is intended that these results shall be accomplished without the loss of life," General Merritt ordered. Further, they issued orders to keep the Filipino *insurrectos* out of Manila, again without bloodshed. To restrain American troops as well as *insurrectos* from shooting Spaniards was close to impossible. Of one further complication the commanders were not aware because of the cut cables; already the United States and Spain had signed an armistice.

The battle for Manila consequently did involve some loss of life. At nine o'clock the American ships opened fire on Fort San Augustín at Malate, impressively damaging it, but hurting no one since it had been evacuated. American troops, making their way along the beach and wading in the water, carefully signaled their position to the warships. Millet reported:

"The moment the shells ceased to batter the fort and to plough up the surrounding territory, the Colorado men streamed up the beach, waded the inlet and scattered all around the fort. It was evidently deserted. The signal men, who had kept along with the advance, left behind them a trail of insulated wire as they went."

This should have been the end of the battle, but the insurgents had been briskly engaging the Spaniards, who were retaliating. A little way in from the beach, General MacArthur met stubborn resistance from a Spanish blockhouse. For several hours the troops skirmished with the Spaniards as they slowly advanced. Millet wrote:

"Leaving the beach under the garden wall of the first barricaded house which the enemy's sharpshooters had occupied we entered the Camino Real behind the high breastwork of the second line of defences. The broad, straight thoroughfare was now busy with our men dashing across by squads from one side to the other and peppering the retreating Spaniards whenever they caught sight of them. Now they climbed into the garden of a pleasant villa, now they dodged among the plantains and behind the wattled fences of the native huts, always advancing and firing. Deliberately and stubbornly the scattered enemy retired from corner to corner, from cover to cover, pausing only to pump out bullets as they went." By noon they were in the plaza of Malate. "Pushing rapidly on up the street we met a civilian who shouted: 'The Spanirads have raised a white flag!'

"Without waiting for more [General Greene], followed by a half dozen of us who were mounted, galloped up the street" into the public promenade of Manila, the Luneta, while Spanish infantrymen fired at them from the city walls.

"In a few minutes we reached a heavy barricade of railway iron across the sea front promenade under the low battery. . . . Here at a small embrasure . . . an officer and a private soldier appeared as we drew near. General Greene asked him if the town had surrendered, and he replied that he did not know, as he had simply been ordered to put up the white flag." As Greene waited to enter Manila, various troop units came up and answered the sporadic Spanish firing. At the bridge over the moat into the walled city stood H Company of the Twenty-third Regulars. Beyond them, stretching down the road for a long distance, were Spanish infantry. Captain O'Connor of the Twenty-third Regulars explained "that this was the force retreating from Santa Ana and that he had halted them and refused to let them enter the town until he had been ordered to do so." In several directions there was a confusing array of Spanish troops in white and Americans in brown. There was also "a continuous sound of firing." "A single careless shot might start an annihilating fire and bring about a terrible disaster."

General Greene soon ended the tension. In the distance he saw the main body of American troops advancing. Ordering them to hold the gates, he directed the Spanish officers to march their troops into Manila. Two men in livery driving a carriage arrived, bringing a note to Greene informing him that the navy and army representatives had gone ashore and were negotiating the surrender. Greene got into their carriage. He later reported:

"I returned within the walls with the messenger. . . . The Spaniards had drawn up terms of surrender. . . . I then returned to the troops outside the walls and sent Captain Birkhimer's battalion of the Third Artillery down the Paco Road to prevent any insurgents from entering. Feeling satisfied that there would be no attack from the Spanish troops lining the walls, I put the regiments in motion toward the bridges, brushing aside a considerable force of insurgents who had penetrated the city . . . and were in the main street with their flag, expecting to march into the walled city and plant it on the walls. . . . I marched down the river to the captain of the port's office, where I ordered the Spanish flag hauled down and the American flag raised in its place."

Manila was in American hands; thousands of Spanish troops milling around inside the walled city were under their protection, and Aguinaldo's men were firmly kept out. On the following day, the formal articles of capitulation were signed. General Merritt established the machinery of military government, but he and Dewey queried Washington how far they should go in resisting the insurgent pressure for joint occupation of Manila. An immediate reply was sent on August 17:

"The President directs that there must be no joint occupation with the insurgents. . . . The insurgents and all others must recognize the military occupation and authority of the United States. . . . Use whatever means in your judgment are necessary to this end. All law-abiding people must be treated alike."

"The insurgents," Millet reported, "exasperated at their failure to participate in the occupation of the town proper, busied themselves at once in turning the Spanish earthworks into offensive positions, dug many new trenches and made active preparations for renewing the siege of the town, always with the excuse that when the United States troops evacuated Manila they might be ready to complete their conquest of the hated race. At Tondo, the northwesterly district of the town, they established their line within revolver shot of our barracks, and in many quarters of the town there was constantly recurring dispute as to which force had the right to occupy certain streets."

The campaign to liberate the oppressed victims of Spanish colonialism had come to an end; the seeds of the new Philippine insurrection had been planted.

16

Victory— and Death

Less than four months after war had been declared, on Friday, August 12, 1898, at half past four, Secretary of State William R. Day and the French ambassador, Jules Cambon, acting on behalf of Spain, signed a peace protocol ending hostilities. President McKinley immediately proclaimed an armistice.

It may have disappointed a few soldiers in Puerto Rico and the Philippines, anxious for more glory, but it came too late for many others in army camps in both the United States and Cuba, ravished by disease. Bad food, impossible sanitation, and continuous rains had led to outbreaks of typhoid and dysentery among the depressed and demoralized men, left behind and forgotten by the public, in the army camps of Florida, Virginia, and Tennessee.

Yellow fever added to the crisis in Cuba during the days immediately following the surrender of Santiago, but most of the malnourished, wretched, fever-racked troops were suffering not from it, but from malaria and dysentery. The chief surgeon of the United States Volunteers, Dr. Nicholas Senn, reported in the *Journal of the American Medical Association:*

"Typhoid fever, which prevailed in all of our large camps before the army sailed for Cuba, soon gained a firm foothold at the seat of war and did its share in increasing the mortality and in shattering the efficiency of the service. Amebic dysentery and diarrhea, the two greatest enemies of the Spanish army, thinned out our ranks and crowded our imperfectly equipped hospitals. . . .

"Those who saw the different regiments leave our State and national camps would find it difficult to recognize and identify the soldiers of the Cuban campaign. The men left in excellent spirits. Most of them return as mere shadows of their former selves. The pale faces, the sunken eyes, the staggering gait and the emaciated forms show only too plainly the effects of climate and disease. Many of them are wrecks for life, others are candidates for a premature grave, and hundreds will require the most careful attention and treatment before they regain the vigor they lost in Cuba."

When Secretary Alger received the frightening news that there was yellow fever among the soldiers in Cuba, he cabled, "The troops must all be put in camps as comfortable as they can be made and remain, I suppose, until the fever has had its run."

This was black news for the Fifth Corps. Captain Herbert O. Hicks and Corporal Fred A. Simmons of Company M, Second Massachusetts Infantry, diagnosed the maladies of their unit:

"The men answering surgeons' calls would get salts one morning and the next castor oil. It was no strange sight, at reveille, to see men crawl out of their tents, try to stand up but fall like logs before any one could reach them. This was one of the stages of malaria. Home sickness was another and perhaps the worst feature we had to deal with. With nothing to do the men had plenty of time to think. This is what wrought the mis-

Nurses aboard, Relief, Siboney

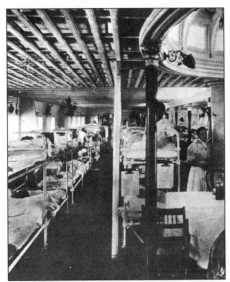

Ward Three

Camp Wikoff, Montauk Point, New York

Rough Riders on parade drill

T.R. giving orders to Gordon Johnston

chief. A soldier must not think. The men who tried the hardest to keep up, in most cases, were the best off."

Cautiously, Secretary Alger prepared a camp to which to return the soldiers, at Montauk Point, on the far tip of Long Island, a full 125 miles from New York City. But it was only on August 3, when well over four thousand of General Shafter's command were on sick report, that he finally authorized return of the troops to isolated Montauk. The next day, Secretary Alger read in the newspapers a round-robin to General Shafter signed by Colonel Roosevelt, by this time a brigade commander, and seven generals:

"The army is disabled by malarial fever to the extent that its efficiency is destroyed, and . . . it is in a condition to be practically entirely destroyed by an epidemic of yellow fever, which is sure to come in the near future. . . .

"This army must be moved at once, or perish. As the army can be safely moved now, the persons responsible for preventing such a move will be responsible for the unnecessary loss of many thousands of lives."

Throughout the country the effect was to give credit to Colonel Roosevelt for the orders that had already been issued and to add new luster to his remarkable reputation.

The first transports began to load almost immediately—and the Rough Riders sailed out of Santiago harbor on the *Miama* on August 8. Trooper J. O. Wells wrote in his diary:

"As we sailed down the bay, we could plainly see the batteries on the shore, the sunken *Merrimac* and the *Reina Mercedes* with her guns pointing skyward as she lay on her side. The cliffs on each side were lined with formidable looking guns, but above them floated the stars and stripes.

"Our trip north was made under as pleasant conditions as a crowded, stuffy transport would allow. The sea was calm and the fresh, cool, sea breezes gave us new life and vigor. As we steamed slowly northward new strength came day by day.

"On the 14th we sighted land off the Jersey coast and the next morning we anchored off Montauk Point. Not until then did we learn that the Peace Protocol had been signed and that hostilities had ceased. . . .

"After being inspected by quarantine officers, we landed and marched to the 'detention camp.' After four days in the 'detention camp' with no signs of 'yellow fever' we went across Long Island to our permanent quarters, where we got good food and comfortable tents."

Some 514 soldiers, less fortunate than Trooper Wells, died of disease in Cuba; half again as many died on transports or after arriving at Montauk. With the battles over, newspapers turned for fresh excitement to Camp Wikoff at Montauk Point and raged against the mistreatment and neglect of the ill and convalescent soldiers, and even the desecration of the dead. *Harper's Weekly* published a letter from a young woman who described soldiers starving, thirsty, and cold:

"From in front of one of the tents a tall, thin, shaky figure got slowly up and came toward us. I thought, 'Good heavens, I hope that's not *Jack!* . . .

"We rushed up to him, and he caught hold of us as though he would never let go again. Mamma came up just then, and Jack smiled at her, and the next moment rolled over at our feet in a dead faint. . . . Jack was a *well man*, and was to go on guard that night."

Far from being neglected on a lonely, sandy point, the returned troops were in a national show window at Camp Wikoff. On September 3, President McKinley, accompanied by Vice-President Garret A. Hobart, visited them. "I am glad to meet you," President McKinley declared, and in rolling phrases, perfected through years of oration before G. A. R. Camp-Fires, he proclaimed, "You have come home after two months of severe campaigning, which has embraced assault and siege and battle, so brilliant in achievement, so far-reaching in results as to command the unstinted praise of all your countrymen."

But it was Colonel Roosevelt, fresh, young, and exciting, who commanded the most enthusiasm among the newspapermen at Camp Wikoff. Surrounded by the Rough Riders, who back on their mounts provided a sort of continuous rodeo, he seemed engaged in a preliminary campaign for the nomination as governor of New York. Soon he and his men were mustered out, and in the fall as candidate he went on a whistle-stop tour of the state, appearing on the rear platform with the Rough Rider bugler behind him. For Roosevelt, the path was short from San Juan Hill to the White House. As he thought over the events of the previous months before he left Montauk, he wrote his friend John Hay, who had just been elevated to secretary of state, "Yes, I was right to go, although I suppose, at bottom I was merely following my instinct instead of my reason."

There must have been many others who felt as sure as Roosevelt that it had been right to go, and who like him reaped the just rewards of heroism and fortitude. There was, for example, Trooper Cosby of the Rough Riders, convalescing from his wounds, who had been promoted to assistant adjutant general with the rank of captain. A dispatch from Bar Harbor, Maine, August 23, 1898, declared that he was "the most 'observed of all observers' at the Malvern ball last night. . . . He was lionized in a manner that eclipsed even the recent reception of the Count of Turin."

Still others could not have been as sure as Roosevelt and Cosby. Perhaps some of the equally courageous Negro troops, for example, trudging into the detention camp on their return from Cuba. They had suffered so much, yet had received so little credit. And all those ill and even dying who had never left the camps in the United States—as seriously disabled by disease as their much-lauded fellow soldiers who had been hit by Spanish bullets.

And then there were all the troops which had sailed to the Philippines. If any of them had been disappointed over the quick end to the fighting in August, they soon had their wish for more excitement granted.

There was no speedy hero's return for them. Rather there were months of tense occupation as the spirit of the American public shaped President McKinley's decision toward annexation of the Philippines. As in Cuba, the liberating army quickly came to fraternize with the defeated Spanish soldiers and to share their scorn for the colonists as inferior people. While a bitter debate over annexation split the Senate and the American people, Aguinaldo and the Filipino patriots on February 4 launched a vehement assault against the occupying forces in Manila. The Senate ratified the treaty with Spain; the American people heeded Rudyard Kipling's poetic charge that they should pick up the "White Man's burden."

For the troops this meant embarking upon a long and difficult war against the Filipino guerrillas which dragged out into a more costly conflict than the Spanish-American War. By the time it came to an end three years later, hundred of Americans and thousands of Filipinos had lost their lives, and the American troops had desperately resorted to the "water cure" and the other cruel tortures of their Spanish predecessors in combating the guerrillas. This was a sad prelude to the establishment of a model colonial administration and a slow preparation of the Filipinos for self-government.

The insurrection did little to mar the great victory celebrations when Admiral Dewey finally returned home in September 1899 to be paraded under an enormous victory arch on Fifth Avenue and to receive from President McKinley in front of the Capitol a sword voted to him by Congress.

The victory arch was made of plaster. Before it could be replaced with marble, the excitement and enthusiasm of the American people gradually faded. The arch slowly disintegrated, and finally was torn down. What Hay had called "the splendid little war" in the summer of 1898 became an almost forgotten war as the United States proceeded into the new challenges of the twentieth century.

Three wars and three score years later, a relative handful of old men still remembered the exploits of their youth, and rightfully resented any depreciation of them. A past national commander of the United Spanish War Veterans, Charles Barefoot, told his appreciative fellow veterans in 1952, "Let me say to you, it was no tin-foil war we were fighting back there."

Victory arch on Fifth Avenue

Bibliography

A most readable, satiric, and thought-provoking account of the Spanish-American War is Walter Millis, *Martial Spirit* (New York, 1931). Also readable and satiric but briefer is Gregory Mason, *Remember the Maine* (New York, 1939). The older, classic history of the war, containing long quotations from documents, is French E. Chadwick, *The Relations of the United States and Spain: The Spanish-American War* (2 vols., New York, 1911). On the Cuban campaign, Herbert H. Sargent, *The Campaign of Santiago de Cuba* (3 vols., Chicago, 1907), is useful and Hermann Hagedorn, *The Rough Riders* (New York, 1927), is vivid. I am heavily indebted to the Society of Santiago de Cuba for their fascinating collection of reminiscences, *The Santiago Campaign* (Richmond, Va., 1927). *Harper's Weekly* and *Leslie's Weekly* provide especially good running pictorial and reportorial accounts of the war. The best contemporary picture histories are W. Nephew King, *The Story of the War of 1898* (New York, 1898), and Harper's and Leslie's histories.

On American entrance into the war, see Julius W. Pratt, *Expansionists of 1898* (Baltimore, 1936); Marcus M. Wilkerson, *Public Opinion and the Spanish-American War* (Baton Rouge, La., 1932); Joseph E. Wisan, *The Cuban Crisis as Reflected in the New York Press* (1895–1898) (New York, 1934); and Richard Hofstadter, "Manifest Destiny and the Philippines," in Daniel Aaron, ed., *American in Crisis* (New York, 1952). Especially valuable is Ernest May, "The Spanish-American War as an Irrepressible Conflict," a paper delivered before the Mississippi Valley Historical Association, April 1958. On the trouble with the German squadron, see Thomas A. Bailey, "Dewey and the Germans at Manila Bay," *American Historical Review,* October 1939, 45:59–81.

Among documentary materials are: *Annual Report of the Major-General Commanding the Army.* . . . (Washington, 1898); *Correspondence Relating to the War With Spain* . . . (2 vols., Washington, 1902); *Report of the Commission to Investigate the Conduct of the War Department* . . . (8 vols., Washington, 1900) [Dodge Commission Report]; Office of Naval Intelligence, *War Notes and Information from Abroad* series (Washington, 1898–1900).

From among the vast quantity of writings on the war, I have made use of the following:

Alger, Russell A., *The Spanish-American War* (New York, 1901)

Archibald, James F. J., "The First Engagement of American Troops on Cuban Soil," *Scribner's*, Aug. 1898

Atkins, John Black, *The War in Cuba* (London, 1899)

Bacon, Alexander S., *The Seventy-First at San Juan* (2nd ed., New York, 1900)

Bee, The, 1898

Berryman, John, *Stephen Crane* (New York, 1950)

Bigelow, John, Jr., *Reminiscences of the Santiago Campaign* (New York, 1899)

Bosnal, Stephen, *The Fight for Santiago* (New York, 1899)

Bowe, John, *With the Thirteenth Minnesota* (Minneapolis, 1905)

Calkins, Carlos G., "Historical and Professional Notes on the Naval Campaign of Manila Bay in 1898," *Proceedings of the Naval Institute*, June 1899

Carnes, Cecil, *Jimmy Hare, News Photographer* (New York, 1940)

Cassard, William G., ed., *Battleship Indiana* (New York, 1898)

Chamberlin, Joseph E., "How the Spaniards Fought at Caney," *Scribner's*, Sept. 1898

Chicago Record's War Stories, The (Chicago, 1898)

Churchhill, Winston S., *My Early Life* (London, 1930)

Clayton, Bertram T., "With General Miles in Porto Rico," *The Independent*, March 9, 1899

Coblentz, Edmond D., ed., *William Randolph Hearst, a Portrait in His Own Words* (New York, 1952)

Coursey, W. S., "McKinley as Commander in Chief," *National Magazine*, May 1902

Crane, Stephen, "War Memories," *Anglo-Saxon Review*, Dec. 1899

Crane, Stephen, *Wounds in the Rain* (New York, 1900)

Davis, Richard Harding, *The Cuban and Porto Rican Campaigns* (New York, 1899)

Davis, Richard Harding, "Our War Correspondents in Cuba and Puerto Rico," *Harper's*, May 1899

Deignan, Osborn W., "The Sinking of the Merrimac," *Leslie's*, Jan. 1899

Dewey, Adelbert M., *The Life and Letters of Admiral Dewey* (New York, 1899)

Dewey, George, *Autobiography* (New York, 1913)

Dyler, John P., "Fightin' Joe" *Wheeler* (Baton Rouge, La., 1941)

Eberle, Edward W., "The 'Oregon's' Great Voyage," *Century*, Oct. 1898

Edwards, F. E., *The '98 Campaign of the 6th Massachusetts* (Boston, 1899)

Elmendorf, John E., ed., *The 71st Regiment New York Volunteers in Cuba* (New York, 1899)

Emerson, Edwin, *Rough Rider Stories* (New York, 1900)

Evans, Robley D., *A Sailor's Log* (New York, 1901)

Evans Robley D., and others, "The Story of the Captains," *Century*, May 1899

Fiske, Bradley A., "Personal Recollections of the Battle of Manila," *United Service*, Jan. 1902 *et seq.*

Fiske, Bradley A., "Why We Won at Manila," *Century*, Nov. 1898

Gantenbein, C. U., *Oregon Volunteers in the Spanish War* (Salem, Ore., 1903)

Goode, W. A. M., *With Sampson Through the War* (New York, 1899)

Graham, George E., *Schley and Santiago* (Chicago, 1902)

Greene, Francis V., "The Capture of Manila," *Century*, March–April 1899

Hancock, H. Irving, *What One Man Saw* (New York, 1898)

Harden, Edward W., "Dewey at Manila," *McClure's*, Feb. 1899

Harris, Harry L., and John T. Hilton, *A History of the . . . Second N.J. Volunteers* (Paterson, N. J., 1908)

Healy, Laurin H., and Luis Kutner, *The Admiral* (Chicago, 1944)

Hemment, John C., *Cannon and Camera* (New York, 1898)

Hicks, Herbert O., and Fred A. Simmons, *Company M* (Adams, Mass., 1899)

History of Troop "A," New York Cavalry, U.S.V. . . . in the Spanish-American War, The (New York, 1899)

Hobson, Richmond P., *The Sinking of the Merrimac* (New York, 1899)

[Huntington], "A Trooper's Diary," *Outlook*, July 30, 1898, *et seq.*

Illustrated London News, 1898

Jane, Frederick T., "The 'Maine' Disaster and After," *Fortnightly Review*, April 1898

Keller, Peter, "The Rescue of Admiral Cervera," *Harper's*, April 1899

Kennan, George, *Campaigning in Cuba* (New York, 1899)

Lee, Arthur H., "The Regulars at El Caney," *Scribner's*, Oct. 1898

Log of the U.S. Gunboat Gloucester (Annapolis, 1899)

Long, John D., *The New American Navy* (2 vols., New York, 1903)

Long, Margaret, ed., *Journal of John D. Long* (Rindge, N. H., 1956)

Loud, George A., and others, "The Battle of Manila Bay," *Century*, Aug. 1898

Mabey, Charles R., *The Utah Batteries* (Salt Lake City, 1900)

McClernand, E. J., *Recollections of the Santiago Campaign* (1922)

McCurdy, F. Allen, and J. Kirk, *Two Rough Riders* (New York, 1902)

McIntosh, Burr, *The Little I Saw of Cuba* (New York, 1899)

Maclay, Edgar Stanton, *Life and Adventures of "Jack" Phillip* (New York, 1903)

Mahan, A. T., *Lessons of the War With Spain* (Boston, 1899)

Marshall, Edward, "The Santiago Campaign," *Scribner's*, Sept. 1898

Mathews, Joseph J., *Reporting the Wars* (Minneapolis, 1957)

Mathews, William, and Dixon Wecter, *Our Soldiers Speak, 1775–1918* (Boston, 1943)

Michelson, Charles, *The Ghost Talks* (New York, 1944)

Miles, Nelson A., *Serving the Republic* (New York, 1911)

Miley, John D., *In Cuba with Shafter* (New York, 1899)

Millet, Frank L., *The Expedition to the Philippines* (New York, 1899)

Mitchell, Donald W., *History of the Modern American Navy* (New York, 1946)

Morison, Elting, *Admiral Sims and the Modern American Navy* (Boston, 1942)

Morison, Elting, ed., *The Letters of Theodore Roosevelt* (vol. 2, Cambridge, Mass., 1951)

Moss, James A., *Memories of the Campaign of Santiago* (San Francisco, 1899)

Musgrave, George C., *Under Three Flags in Cuba* (Boston, 1899)

New York and the War With Spain (Albany, 1903)

New York Times Illustrated Weekly Magazine, 1898

Niemeyer, Harry H., *Yarns of Battery A: With the Artillery-men at Chickamauga and Porto Rico* [n.p., n.d.]

Olcott, Charles S., *The Life of William McKinley* (2 vols., Boston, 1916)

Parker, James, *Schley, Sampson and Cervera* (New York, 1910)

Parker, John H., *History of the Gatling Gun Detachment* (Kansas City, 1898)

Person's War Pictures, 1898

Pershing, John J., "The Campaign of Santiago," in *Under Fire with the Tenth Cavalry* (Chicago, 1902)

Pierce, Frederick E., *Reminiscences of . . . Company L* (Greenfield, Mass., 1900)

Remington, Frederic, "With the Fifth Corps," *Harper's*, Nov. 1898

Roosevelt, Theodore, *The Rough Riders* (New York, 1899)

Sampson, William T., "The Atlantic Fleet in the Spanish War," *Century*, April 1899

Sargent, Nathan, compiler, *Admiral Dewey and the Manila Campaign* (Washington, D.C., 1947)

Schley, Winfield Scott, *Forty-five Years Under the Flag* (New York, 1904)

Senn, Nicholas, *War Correspondence* (Chicago, 1899)

Shafter, William R., "The Capture of Santiago de Cuba," *Century*, Feb. 1899

Sigsbee, Charles D., *The "Maine," An Account of her Destruction in Havana Harbor* (New York, 1899)

Spanish-American War . . . by Eye Witnesses, The (Chicago, 1899)

Spears, John R., "Afloat for News in War Times," *Scribner's*, Oct. 1898

Spears, John R., *Our Navy in the War with Spain* (New York, 1898)

Sprout, H. H. and Margaret, *The Rise of the American Naval Power, 1776–1918* (Princeton, 1939)

Stickney, Joseph L., *War in the Philippines* (Springfield, Mass., 1899)

Titherington, Richard H., "Our War With Spain," *Munsey's*, Oct. 1898 *et seq.*

United Spanish War Veterans, *Annual Report*, 1952

Vincent, George E., ed., *Theodore W. Miller, Rough Rider* (Akron, O., 1899)

"War History in Private Letters," *Outlook*, Aug. 13, 1898, *et. seq.*

Wells, J. O., *Diary of a Rough Rider* (St. Joseph, Mich., 1898?)

Wheeler, Joseph, *The Santiago Campaign* (Boston, 1898)

White, Douglas, "The Capture of the Island of Guam, the True Story," *Overland Monthly*, March 1900

White, William Allen, "When Johnny Went Marching Out," *McClure's*, June 1898

Wilson, James Harrison, *Under the Old Flag* (2 vols., New York, 1912)

Photo Credits

All illustrations courtesy the National Archives, Still Picture Branch, unless otherwise noted.

1. Remember the Maine: 5: (upper) Library of Congress; (lower) Van der Weyde, Theodore Roosevelt collection; 6: (upper) New York *World*, February 17, 1898. **2. The Battle of Manila Bay:** 17: (upper) George Grantham, #4046, Official U.S. Navy Photograph; 18: (upper) #534, Official U.S. Navy Photograph; (lower) #18190, Official U.S. Navy Photograph. **3. As Johnny Went Marching Off:** 31: (upper) Elmendorf, Theodore Roosevelt collection; (middle) Elmendorf, Roosevelt collection; (lower) Elmendorf, Roosevelt collection; 34: (upper) #608, Official U.S. Navy Photograph; (lower) Elmendorf, Roosevelt collection. **4. Hunting the Spanish Fleet:** 46: (upper) Elmendorf, TR collection. **6. Daiquiri Beachhead:** 70: William Dinwiddie, Library of Congress. **7. Skirmish at Las Guasimas:** 89: *Leslie's Weekly*, Sept. 8, 1898, 87:188,193; 90: Burr McIntosh, TR collection. **8. Assault on El Caney:** 108: *Leslie's Weekly*, Oct. 20, 1898, 87:813. **9. Up San Juan Hill:** 113: Library of Congress; 123: (lower) William Dinwiddie, Library of Congress; 129: (upper) W.N. King, *The Story of the War of 1898*, 235; 130: (upper) William Dinwiddie, Library of Congress. **10. A Precarious Toehold:** 141: TR collection. **12. A Fourth of July Present:** 173: W.N. King, *The Story of the War of 1898*, 299; 178: From sketch by C.M. Sheldon, *Leslie's Weekly*, Aug. 25, 1898, 87:141. **13. Siege of Santiago:** 187: *Leslie's Weekly*, Aug. 25, 1898, 87:149. **15. Expedition to the Phillipines:** 218: *Harper's Weekly*, July 30, 1898, 42:753. **16. Victory—and Death:** 232: (upper) Elmendorf, Theodore Roosevelt collection; (lower) Elmendorf, Roosevelt collection; 237: Elmendorf, Roosevelt collection.

Index